C-1411   CAREER EXAMINATION SERIES

This is your
PASSBOOK for...

Food Service Supervisor

Test Preparation Study Guide
Questions & Answers

COPYRIGHT NOTICE

This book is SOLELY intended for, is sold ONLY to, and its use is RESTRICTED to individual, bona fide applicants or candidates who qualify by virtue of having seriously filed applications for appropriate license, certificate, professional and/or promotional advancement, higher school matriculation, scholarship, or other legitimate requirements of education and/or governmental authorities.

This book is NOT intended for use, class instruction, tutoring, training, duplication, copying, reprinting, excerption, or adaptation, etc., by:

1) Other publishers
2) Proprietors and/or Instructors of "Coaching" and/or Preparatory Courses
3) Personnel and/or Training Divisions of commercial, industrial, and governmental organizations
4) Schools, colleges, or universities and/or their departments and staffs, including teachers and other personnel
5) Testing Agencies or Bureaus
6) Study groups which seek by the purchase of a single volume to copy and/or duplicate and/or adapt this material for use by the group as a whole without having purchased individual volumes for each of the members of the group
7) Et al.

Such persons would be in violation of appropriate Federal and State statutes.

PROVISION OF LICENSING AGREEMENTS – Recognized educational, commercial, industrial, and governmental institutions and organizations, and others legitimately engaged in educational pursuits, including training, testing, and measurement activities, may address request for a licensing agreement to the copyright owners, who will determine whether, and under what conditions, including fees and charges, the materials in this book may be used them. In other words, a licensing facility exists for the legitimate use of the material in this book on other than an individual basis. However, it is asseverated and affirmed here that the material in this book CANNOT be used without the receipt of the express permission of such a licensing agreement from the Publishers. Inquiries re licensing should be addressed to the company, attention rights and permissions department.

All rights reserved, including the right of reproduction in whole or in part, in any form or by any means, electronic or mechanical, including photocopying, recording, or by any information storage and retrieval system, without permission in writing from the Publisher.

Copyright © 2024 by
National Learning Corporation

212 Michael Drive, Syosset, NY 11791
(516) 921-8888 • www.passbooks.com
E-mail: info@passbooks.com

PUBLISHED IN THE UNITED STATES OF AMERICA

PASSBOOK® SERIES

THE *PASSBOOK® SERIES* has been created to prepare applicants and candidates for the ultimate academic battlefield – the examination room.

At some time in our lives, each and every one of us may be required to take an examination – for validation, matriculation, admission, qualification, registration, certification, or licensure.

Based on the assumption that every applicant or candidate has met the basic formal educational standards, has taken the required number of courses, and read the necessary texts, the *PASSBOOK® SERIES* furnishes the one special preparation which may assure passing with confidence, instead of failing with insecurity. Examination questions – together with answers – are furnished as the basic vehicle for study so that the mysteries of the examination and its compounding difficulties may be eliminated or diminished by a sure method.

This book is meant to help you pass your examination provided that you qualify and are serious in your objective.

The entire field is reviewed through the huge store of content information which is succinctly presented through a provocative and challenging approach – the question-and-answer method.

A climate of success is established by furnishing the correct answers at the end of each test.

You soon learn to recognize types of questions, forms of questions, and patterns of questioning. You may even begin to anticipate expected outcomes.

You perceive that many questions are repeated or adapted so that you can gain acute insights, which may enable you to score many sure points.

You learn how to confront new questions, or types of questions, and to attack them confidently and work out the correct answers.

You note objectives and emphases, and recognize pitfalls and dangers, so that you may make positive educational adjustments.

Moreover, you are kept fully informed in relation to new concepts, methods, practices, and directions in the field.

You discover that you are actually taking the examination all the time: you are preparing for the examination by "taking" an examination, not by reading extraneous and/or supererogatory textbooks.

In short, this PASSBOOK®, used directedly, should be an important factor in helping you to pass your test.

FOOD SERVICE SUPERVISOR

DUTIES

An employee in this class supervises or monitors the planning, preparation and serving of meals to a large group of people. The incumbent may be directly responsible for food service in an institution, or may monitor a contracted program for the elderly at several different sites. The incumbent is responsible for all phases of food service, including cost control, record keeping and supervision. Does related work as required.

SCOPE OF THE EXAMINATION

The multiple-choice test covers knowledge, skills and abilities in such areas as:

1. Large-scale food preparation and service;
2. Food service management principles and practices;
3. Food sanitation and storage;
4. Menu planning, nutrition and dietetics;
5. Supervision and training; and
6. Office record keeping.

HOW TO TAKE A TEST

I. YOU MUST PASS AN EXAMINATION

A. *WHAT EVERY CANDIDATE SHOULD KNOW*

Examination applicants often ask us for help in preparing for the written test. What can I study in advance? What kinds of questions will be asked? How will the test be given? How will the papers be graded?

As an applicant for a civil service examination, you may be wondering about some of these things. Our purpose here is to suggest effective methods of advance study and to describe civil service examinations.

Your chances for success on this examination can be increased if you know how to prepare. Those "pre-examination jitters" can be reduced if you know what to expect. You can even experience an adventure in good citizenship if you know why civil service exams are given.

B. *WHY ARE CIVIL SERVICE EXAMINATIONS GIVEN?*

Civil service examinations are important to you in two ways. As a citizen, you want public jobs filled by employees who know how to do their work. As a job seeker, you want a fair chance to compete for that job on an equal footing with other candidates. The best-known means of accomplishing this two-fold goal is the competitive examination.

Exams are widely publicized throughout the nation. They may be administered for jobs in federal, state, city, municipal, town or village governments or agencies.

Any citizen may apply, with some limitations, such as the age or residence of applicants. Your experience and education may be reviewed to see whether you meet the requirements for the particular examination. When these requirements exist, they are reasonable and applied consistently to all applicants. Thus, a competitive examination may cause you some uneasiness now, but it is your privilege and safeguard.

C. *HOW ARE CIVIL SERVICE EXAMS DEVELOPED?*

Examinations are carefully written by trained technicians who are specialists in the field known as "psychological measurement," in consultation with recognized authorities in the field of work that the test will cover. These experts recommend the subject matter areas or skills to be tested; only those knowledges or skills important to your success on the job are included. The most reliable books and source materials available are used as references. Together, the experts and technicians judge the difficulty level of the questions.

Test technicians know how to phrase questions so that the problem is clearly stated. Their ethics do not permit "trick" or "catch" questions. Questions may have been tried out on sample groups, or subjected to statistical analysis, to determine their usefulness.

Written tests are often used in combination with performance tests, ratings of training and experience, and oral interviews. All of these measures combine to form the best-known means of finding the right person for the right job.

II. HOW TO PASS THE WRITTEN TEST

A. NATURE OF THE EXAMINATION

To prepare intelligently for civil service examinations, you should know how they differ from school examinations you have taken. In school you were assigned certain definite pages to read or subjects to cover. The examination questions were quite detailed and usually emphasized memory. Civil service exams, on the other hand, try to discover your present ability to perform the duties of a position, plus your potentiality to learn these duties. In other words, a civil service exam attempts to predict how successful you will be. Questions cover such a broad area that they cannot be as minute and detailed as school exam questions.

In the public service similar kinds of work, or positions, are grouped together in one "class." This process is known as *position-classification*. All the positions in a class are paid according to the salary range for that class. One class title covers all of these positions, and they are all tested by the same examination.

B. FOUR BASIC STEPS

1) Study the announcement

How, then, can you know what subjects to study? Our best answer is: "Learn as much as possible about the class of positions for which you've applied." The exam will test the knowledge, skills and abilities needed to do the work.

Your most valuable source of information about the position you want is the official exam announcement. This announcement lists the training and experience qualifications. Check these standards and apply only if you come reasonably close to meeting them.

The brief description of the position in the examination announcement offers some clues to the subjects which will be tested. Think about the job itself. Review the duties in your mind. Can you perform them, or are there some in which you are rusty? Fill in the blank spots in your preparation.

Many jurisdictions preview the written test in the exam announcement by including a section called "Knowledge and Abilities Required," "Scope of the Examination," or some similar heading. Here you will find out specifically what fields will be tested.

2) Review your own background

Once you learn in general what the position is all about, and what you need to know to do the work, ask yourself which subjects you already know fairly well and which need improvement. You may wonder whether to concentrate on improving your strong areas or on building some background in your fields of weakness. When the announcement has specified "some knowledge" or "considerable knowledge," or has used adjectives like "beginning principles of…" or "advanced … methods," you can get a clue as to the number and difficulty of questions to be asked in any given field. More questions, and hence broader coverage, would be included for those subjects which are more important in the work. Now weigh your strengths and weaknesses against the job requirements and prepare accordingly.

3) Determine the level of the position

Another way to tell how intensively you should prepare is to understand the level of the job for which you are applying. Is it the entering level? In other words, is this the position in which beginners in a field of work are hired? Or is it an intermediate or advanced level? Sometimes this is indicated by such words as "Junior" or "Senior" in the class title. Other jurisdictions use Roman numerals to designate the level – Clerk I, Clerk II, for example. The word "Supervisor" sometimes appears in the title. If the level is not indicated by the title, check the description of duties. Will you be working under very close supervision, or will you have responsibility for independent decisions in this work?

4) Choose appropriate study materials

Now that you know the subjects to be examined and the relative amount of each subject to be covered, you can choose suitable study materials. For beginning level jobs, or even advanced ones, if you have a pronounced weakness in some aspect of your training, read a modern, standard textbook in that field. Be sure it is up to date and has general coverage. Such books are normally available at your library, and the librarian will be glad to help you locate one. For entry-level positions, questions of appropriate difficulty are chosen – neither highly advanced questions, nor those too simple. Such questions require careful thought but not advanced training.

If the position for which you are applying is technical or advanced, you will read more advanced, specialized material. If you are already familiar with the basic principles of your field, elementary textbooks would waste your time. Concentrate on advanced textbooks and technical periodicals. Think through the concepts and review difficult problems in your field.

These are all general sources. You can get more ideas on your own initiative, following these leads. For example, training manuals and publications of the government agency which employs workers in your field can be useful, particularly for technical and professional positions. A letter or visit to the government department involved may result in more specific study suggestions, and certainly will provide you with a more definite idea of the exact nature of the position you are seeking.

III. KINDS OF TESTS

Tests are used for purposes other than measuring knowledge and ability to perform specified duties. For some positions, it is equally important to test ability to make adjustments to new situations or to profit from training. In others, basic mental abilities not dependent on information are essential. Questions which test these things may not appear as pertinent to the duties of the position as those which test for knowledge and information. Yet they are often highly important parts of a fair examination. For very general questions, it is almost impossible to help you direct your study efforts. What we can do is to point out some of the more common of these general abilities needed in public service positions and describe some typical questions.

1) General information

Broad, general information has been found useful for predicting job success in some kinds of work. This is tested in a variety of ways, from vocabulary lists to questions about current events. Basic background in some field of work, such as sociology or economics, may be sampled in a group of questions. Often these are principles which have become familiar to most persons through exposure rather than through formal training. It is difficult to advise you how to study for these questions; being alert to the world around you is our best suggestion.

2) Verbal ability

An example of an ability needed in many positions is verbal or language ability. Verbal ability is, in brief, the ability to use and understand words. Vocabulary and grammar tests are typical measures of this ability. Reading comprehension or paragraph interpretation questions are common in many kinds of civil service tests. You are given a paragraph of written material and asked to find its central meaning.

3) Numerical ability

Number skills can be tested by the familiar arithmetic problem, by checking paired lists of numbers to see which are alike and which are different, or by interpreting charts and graphs. In the latter test, a graph may be printed in the test booklet which you are asked to use as the basis for answering questions.

4) Observation

A popular test for law-enforcement positions is the observation test. A picture is shown to you for several minutes, then taken away. Questions about the picture test your ability to observe both details and larger elements.

5) Following directions

In many positions in the public service, the employee must be able to carry out written instructions dependably and accurately. You may be given a chart with several columns, each column listing a variety of information. The questions require you to carry out directions involving the information given in the chart.

6) Skills and aptitudes

Performance tests effectively measure some manual skills and aptitudes. When the skill is one in which you are trained, such as typing or shorthand, you can practice. These tests are often very much like those given in business school or high school courses. For many of the other skills and aptitudes, however, no short-time preparation can be made. Skills and abilities natural to you or that you have developed throughout your lifetime are being tested.

Many of the general questions just described provide all the data needed to answer the questions and ask you to use your reasoning ability to find the answers. Your best preparation for these tests, as well as for tests of facts and ideas, is to be at your physical and mental best. You, no doubt, have your own methods of getting into an exam-taking mood and keeping "in shape." The next section lists some ideas on this subject.

IV. KINDS OF QUESTIONS

Only rarely is the "essay" question, which you answer in narrative form, used in civil service tests. Civil service tests are usually of the short-answer type. Full instructions for answering these questions will be given to you at the examination. But in case this is your first experience with short-answer questions and separate answer sheets, here is what you need to know:

1) Multiple-choice Questions

Most popular of the short-answer questions is the "multiple choice" or "best answer" question. It can be used, for example, to test for factual knowledge, ability to solve problems or judgment in meeting situations found at work.

A multiple-choice question is normally one of three types—
- It can begin with an incomplete statement followed by several possible endings. You are to find the one ending which *best* completes the statement, although some of the others may not be entirely wrong.
- It can also be a complete statement in the form of a question which is answered by choosing one of the statements listed.

- It can be in the form of a problem – again you select the best answer.

Here is an example of a multiple-choice question with a discussion which should give you some clues as to the method for choosing the right answer:

When an employee has a complaint about his assignment, the action which will *best* help him overcome his difficulty is to
- A. discuss his difficulty with his coworkers
- B. take the problem to the head of the organization
- C. take the problem to the person who gave him the assignment
- D. say nothing to anyone about his complaint

In answering this question, you should study each of the choices to find which is best. Consider choice "A" – Certainly an employee may discuss his complaint with fellow employees, but no change or improvement can result, and the complaint remains unresolved. Choice "B" is a poor choice since the head of the organization probably does not know what assignment you have been given, and taking your problem to him is known as "going over the head" of the supervisor. The supervisor, or person who made the assignment, is the person who can clarify it or correct any injustice. Choice "C" is, therefore, correct. To say nothing, as in choice "D," is unwise. Supervisors have and interest in knowing the problems employees are facing, and the employee is seeking a solution to his problem.

2) True/False Questions

The "true/false" or "right/wrong" form of question is sometimes used. Here a complete statement is given. Your job is to decide whether the statement is right or wrong.

SAMPLE: A roaming cell-phone call to a nearby city costs less than a non-roaming call to a distant city.

This statement is wrong, or false, since roaming calls are more expensive.

This is not a complete list of all possible question forms, although most of the others are variations of these common types. You will always get complete directions for answering questions. Be sure you understand *how* to mark your answers – ask questions until you do.

V. RECORDING YOUR ANSWERS

Computer terminals are used more and more today for many different kinds of exams.
For an examination with very few applicants, you may be told to record your answers in the test booklet itself. Separate answer sheets are much more common. If this separate answer sheet is to be scored by machine – and this is often the case – it is highly important that you mark your answers correctly in order to get credit.
An electronic scoring machine is often used in civil service offices because of the speed with which papers can be scored. Machine-scored answer sheets must be marked with a pencil, which will be given to you. This pencil has a high graphite content which responds to the electronic scoring machine. As a matter of fact, stray dots may register as answers, so do not let your pencil rest on the answer sheet while you are pondering the correct answer. Also, if your pencil lead breaks or is otherwise defective, ask for another.

Since the answer sheet will be dropped in a slot in the scoring machine, be careful not to bend the corners or get the paper crumpled.

The answer sheet normally has five vertical columns of numbers, with 30 numbers to a column. These numbers correspond to the question numbers in your test booklet. After each number, going across the page are four or five pairs of dotted lines. These short dotted lines have small letters or numbers above them. The first two pairs may also have a "T" or "F" above the letters. This indicates that the first two pairs only are to be used if the questions are of the true-false type. If the questions are multiple choice, disregard the "T" and "F" and pay attention only to the small letters or numbers.

Answer your questions in the manner of the sample that follows:

32. The largest city in the United States is
    A. Washington, D.C.
    B. New York City
    C. Chicago
    D. Detroit
    E. San Francisco

1) Choose the answer you think is best. (New York City is the largest, so "B" is correct.)
2) Find the row of dotted lines numbered the same as the question you are answering. (Find row number 32)
3) Find the pair of dotted lines corresponding to the answer. (Find the pair of lines under the mark "B.")
4) Make a solid black mark between the dotted lines.

VI. BEFORE THE TEST

Common sense will help you find procedures to follow to get ready for an examination. Too many of us, however, overlook these sensible measures. Indeed, nervousness and fatigue have been found to be the most serious reasons why applicants fail to do their best on civil service tests. Here is a list of reminders:

- Begin your preparation early – Don't wait until the last minute to go scurrying around for books and materials or to find out what the position is all about.
- Prepare continuously – An hour a night for a week is better than an all-night cram session. This has been definitely established. What is more, a night a week for a month will return better dividends than crowding your study into a shorter period of time.
- Locate the place of the exam – You have been sent a notice telling you when and where to report for the examination. If the location is in a different town or otherwise unfamiliar to you, it would be well to inquire the best route and learn something about the building.
- Relax the night before the test – Allow your mind to rest. Do not study at all that night. Plan some mild recreation or diversion; then go to bed early and get a good night's sleep.
- Get up early enough to make a leisurely trip to the place for the test – This way unforeseen events, traffic snarls, unfamiliar buildings, etc. will not upset you.
- Dress comfortably – A written test is not a fashion show. You will be known by number and not by name, so wear something comfortable.

- Leave excess paraphernalia at home – Shopping bags and odd bundles will get in your way. You need bring only the items mentioned in the official notice you received; usually everything you need is provided. Do not bring reference books to the exam. They will only confuse those last minutes and be taken away from you when in the test room.
- Arrive somewhat ahead of time – If because of transportation schedules you must get there very early, bring a newspaper or magazine to take your mind off yourself while waiting.
- Locate the examination room – When you have found the proper room, you will be directed to the seat or part of the room where you will sit. Sometimes you are given a sheet of instructions to read while you are waiting. Do not fill out any forms until you are told to do so; just read them and be prepared.
- Relax and prepare to listen to the instructions
- If you have any physical problem that may keep you from doing your best, be sure to tell the test administrator. If you are sick or in poor health, you really cannot do your best on the exam. You can come back and take the test some other time.

VII. AT THE TEST

The day of the test is here and you have the test booklet in your hand. The temptation to get going is very strong. Caution! There is more to success than knowing the right answers. You must know how to identify your papers and understand variations in the type of short-answer question used in this particular examination. Follow these suggestions for maximum results from your efforts:

1) Cooperate with the monitor

The test administrator has a duty to create a situation in which you can be as much at ease as possible. He will give instructions, tell you when to begin, check to see that you are marking your answer sheet correctly, and so on. He is not there to guard you, although he will see that your competitors do not take unfair advantage. He wants to help you do your best.

2) Listen to all instructions

Don't jump the gun! Wait until you understand all directions. In most civil service tests you get more time than you need to answer the questions. So don't be in a hurry. Read each word of instructions until you clearly understand the meaning. Study the examples, listen to all announcements and follow directions. Ask questions if you do not understand what to do.

3) Identify your papers

Civil service exams are usually identified by number only. You will be assigned a number; you must not put your name on your test papers. Be sure to copy your number correctly. Since more than one exam may be given, copy your exact examination title.

4) Plan your time

Unless you are told that a test is a "speed" or "rate of work" test, speed itself is usually not important. Time enough to answer all the questions will be provided, but this does not mean that you have all day. An overall time limit has been set. Divide the total time (in minutes) by the number of questions to determine the approximate time you have for each question.

5) Do not linger over difficult questions

If you come across a difficult question, mark it with a paper clip (useful to have along) and come back to it when you have been through the booklet. One caution if you do this – be sure to skip a number on your answer sheet as well. Check often to be sure that you have not lost your place and that you are marking in the row numbered the same as the question you are answering.

6) Read the questions

Be sure you know what the question asks! Many capable people are unsuccessful because they failed to *read* the questions correctly.

7) Answer all questions

Unless you have been instructed that a penalty will be deducted for incorrect answers, it is better to guess than to omit a question.

8) Speed tests

It is often better NOT to guess on speed tests. It has been found that on timed tests people are tempted to spend the last few seconds before time is called in marking answers at random – without even reading them – in the hope of picking up a few extra points. To discourage this practice, the instructions may warn you that your score will be "corrected" for guessing. That is, a penalty will be applied. The incorrect answers will be deducted from the correct ones, or some other penalty formula will be used.

9) Review your answers

If you finish before time is called, go back to the questions you guessed or omitted to give them further thought. Review other answers if you have time.

10) Return your test materials

If you are ready to leave before others have finished or time is called, take ALL your materials to the monitor and leave quietly. Never take any test material with you. The monitor can discover whose papers are not complete, and taking a test booklet may be grounds for disqualification.

VIII. EXAMINATION TECHNIQUES

1) Read the general instructions carefully. These are usually printed on the first page of the exam booklet. As a rule, these instructions refer to the timing of the examination; the fact that you should not start work until the signal and must stop work at a signal, etc. If there are any *special* instructions, such as a choice of questions to be answered, make sure that you note this instruction carefully.

2) When you are ready to start work on the examination, that is as soon as the signal has been given, read the instructions to each question booklet, underline any key words or phrases, such as *least, best, outline, describe* and the like. In this way you will tend to answer as requested rather than discover on reviewing your paper that you *listed without describing*, that you selected the *worst* choice rather than the *best* choice, etc.

3) If the examination is of the objective or multiple-choice type – that is, each question will also give a series of possible answers: A, B, C or D, and you are called upon to select the best answer and write the letter next to that answer on your answer paper – it is advisable to start answering each question in turn. There may be anywhere from 50 to 100 such questions in the three or four hours allotted and you can see how much time would be taken if you read through all the questions before beginning to answer any. Furthermore, if you come across a question or group of questions which you know would be difficult to answer, it would undoubtedly affect your handling of all the other questions.

4) If the examination is of the essay type and contains but a few questions, it is a moot point as to whether you should read all the questions before starting to answer any one. Of course, if you are given a choice – say five out of seven and the like – then it is essential to read all the questions so you can eliminate the two that are most difficult. If, however, you are asked to answer all the questions, there may be danger in trying to answer the easiest one first because you may find that you will spend too much time on it. The best technique is to answer the first question, then proceed to the second, etc.

5) Time your answers. Before the exam begins, write down the time it started, then add the time allowed for the examination and write down the time it must be completed, then divide the time available somewhat as follows:
    - If 3-1/2 hours are allowed, that would be 210 minutes. If you have 80 objective-type questions, that would be an average of 2-1/2 minutes per question. Allow yourself no more than 2 minutes per question, or a total of 160 minutes, which will permit about 50 minutes to review.
    - If for the time allotment of 210 minutes there are 7 essay questions to answer, that would average about 30 minutes a question. Give yourself only 25 minutes per question so that you have about 35 minutes to review.

6) The most important instruction is to *read each question* and make sure you know what is wanted. The second most important instruction is to *time yourself properly* so that you answer every question. The third most important instruction is to *answer every question*. Guess if you have to but include something for each question. Remember that you will receive no credit for a blank and will probably receive some credit if you write something in answer to an essay question. If you guess a letter – say "B" for a multiple-choice question – you may have guessed right. If you leave a blank as an answer to a multiple-choice question, the examiners may respect your feelings but it will not add a point to your score. Some exams may penalize you for wrong answers, so in such cases *only*, you may not want to guess unless you have some basis for your answer.

7) Suggestions
    a. Objective-type questions
        1. Examine the question booklet for proper sequence of pages and questions
        2. Read all instructions carefully
        3. Skip any question which seems too difficult; return to it after all other questions have been answered
        4. Apportion your time properly; do not spend too much time on any single question or group of questions

5. Note and underline key words – *all, most, fewest, least, best, worst, same, opposite*, etc.
6. Pay particular attention to negatives
7. Note unusual option, e.g., unduly long, short, complex, different or similar in content to the body of the question
8. Observe the use of "hedging" words – *probably, may, most likely*, etc.
9. Make sure that your answer is put next to the same number as the question
10. Do not second-guess unless you have good reason to believe the second answer is definitely more correct
11. Cross out original answer if you decide another answer is more accurate; do not erase until you are ready to hand your paper in
12. Answer all questions; guess unless instructed otherwise
13. Leave time for review

b. Essay questions
1. Read each question carefully
2. Determine exactly what is wanted. Underline key words or phrases.
3. Decide on outline or paragraph answer
4. Include many different points and elements unless asked to develop any one or two points or elements
5. Show impartiality by giving pros and cons unless directed to select one side only
6. Make and write down any assumptions you find necessary to answer the questions
7. Watch your English, grammar, punctuation and choice of words
8. Time your answers; don't crowd material

8) Answering the essay question

Most essay questions can be answered by framing the specific response around several key words or ideas. Here are a few such key words or ideas:

M's: manpower, materials, methods, money, management
P's: purpose, program, policy, plan, procedure, practice, problems, pitfalls, personnel, public relations

   a. Six basic steps in handling problems:
      1. Preliminary plan and background development
      2. Collect information, data and facts
      3. Analyze and interpret information, data and facts
      4. Analyze and develop solutions as well as make recommendations
      5. Prepare report and sell recommendations
      6. Install recommendations and follow up effectiveness

   b. Pitfalls to avoid
      1. *Taking things for granted* – A statement of the situation does not necessarily imply that each of the elements is necessarily true; for example, a complaint may be invalid and biased so that all that can be taken for granted is that a complaint has been registered

2. *Considering only one side of a situation* – Wherever possible, indicate several alternatives and then point out the reasons you selected the best one
3. *Failing to indicate follow up* – Whenever your answer indicates action on your part, make certain that you will take proper follow-up action to see how successful your recommendations, procedures or actions turn out to be
4. *Taking too long in answering any single question* – Remember to time your answers properly

IX. AFTER THE TEST

Scoring procedures differ in detail among civil service jurisdictions although the general principles are the same. Whether the papers are hand-scored or graded by machine we have described, they are nearly always graded by number. That is, the person who marks the paper knows only the number – never the name – of the applicant. Not until all the papers have been graded will they be matched with names. If other tests, such as training and experience or oral interview ratings have been given, scores will be combined. Different parts of the examination usually have different weights. For example, the written test might count 60 percent of the final grade, and a rating of training and experience 40 percent. In many jurisdictions, veterans will have a certain number of points added to their grades.

After the final grade has been determined, the names are placed in grade order and an eligible list is established. There are various methods for resolving ties between those who get the same final grade – probably the most common is to place first the name of the person whose application was received first. Job offers are made from the eligible list in the order the names appear on it. You will be notified of your grade and your rank as soon as all these computations have been made. This will be done as rapidly as possible.

People who are found to meet the requirements in the announcement are called "eligibles." Their names are put on a list of eligible candidates. An eligible's chances of getting a job depend on how high he stands on this list and how fast agencies are filling jobs from the list.

When a job is to be filled from a list of eligibles, the agency asks for the names of people on the list of eligibles for that job. When the civil service commission receives this request, it sends to the agency the names of the three people highest on this list. Or, if the job to be filled has specialized requirements, the office sends the agency the names of the top three persons who meet these requirements from the general list.

The appointing officer makes a choice from among the three people whose names were sent to him. If the selected person accepts the appointment, the names of the others are put back on the list to be considered for future openings.

That is the rule in hiring from all kinds of eligible lists, whether they are for typist, carpenter, chemist, or something else. For every vacancy, the appointing officer has his choice of any one of the top three eligibles on the list. This explains why the person whose name is on top of the list sometimes does not get an appointment when some of the persons lower on the list do. If the appointing officer chooses the second or third eligible, the No. 1 eligible does not get a job at once, but stays on the list until he is appointed or the list is terminated.

X. HOW TO PASS THE INTERVIEW TEST

The examination for which you applied requires an oral interview test. You have already taken the written test and you are now being called for the interview test – the final part of the formal examination.

You may think that it is not possible to prepare for an interview test and that there are no procedures to follow during an interview. Our purpose is to point out some things you can do in advance that will help you and some good rules to follow and pitfalls to avoid while you are being interviewed.

What is an interview supposed to test?

The written examination is designed to test the technical knowledge and competence of the candidate; the oral is designed to evaluate intangible qualities, not readily measured otherwise, and to establish a list showing the relative fitness of each candidate – as measured against his competitors – for the position sought. Scoring is not on the basis of "right" and "wrong," but on a sliding scale of values ranging from "not passable" to "outstanding." As a matter of fact, it is possible to achieve a relatively low score without a single "incorrect" answer because of evident weakness in the qualities being measured.

Occasionally, an examination may consist entirely of an oral test – either an individual or a group oral. In such cases, information is sought concerning the technical knowledges and abilities of the candidate, since there has been no written examination for this purpose. More commonly, however, an oral test is used to supplement a written examination.

Who conducts interviews?

The composition of oral boards varies among different jurisdictions. In nearly all, a representative of the personnel department serves as chairman. One of the members of the board may be a representative of the department in which the candidate would work. In some cases, "outside experts" are used, and, frequently, a businessman or some other representative of the general public is asked to serve. Labor and management or other special groups may be represented. The aim is to secure the services of experts in the appropriate field.

However the board is composed, it is a good idea (and not at all improper or unethical) to ascertain in advance of the interview who the members are and what groups they represent. When you are introduced to them, you will have some idea of their backgrounds and interests, and at least you will not stutter and stammer over their names.

What should be done before the interview?

While knowledge about the board members is useful and takes some of the surprise element out of the interview, there is other preparation which is more substantive. It *is* possible to prepare for an oral interview – in several ways:

1) Keep a copy of your application and review it carefully before the interview

This may be the only document before the oral board, and the starting point of the interview. Know what education and experience you have listed there, and the sequence and dates of all of it. Sometimes the board will ask you to review the highlights of your experience for them; you should not have to hem and haw doing it.

2) Study the class specification and the examination announcement

Usually, the oral board has one or both of these to guide them. The qualities, characteristics or knowledges required by the position sought are stated in these documents. They offer valuable clues as to the nature of the oral interview. For example, if the job involves supervisory responsibilities, the announcement will usually indicate that knowledge of modern supervisory methods and the qualifications of the candidate as a supervisor will be tested. If so, you can expect such questions, frequently in the form of a hypothetical situation which you are expected to solve. NEVER go into an oral without knowledge of the duties and responsibilities of the job you seek.

3) Think through each qualification required

Try to visualize the kind of questions you would ask if you were a board member. How well could you answer them? Try especially to appraise your own knowledge and background in each area, *measured against the job sought*, and identify any areas in which you are weak. Be critical and realistic – do not flatter yourself.

4) Do some general reading in areas in which you feel you may be weak

For example, if the job involves supervision and your past experience has NOT, some general reading in supervisory methods and practices, particularly in the field of human relations, might be useful. Do NOT study agency procedures or detailed manuals. The oral board will be testing your understanding and capacity, not your memory.

5) Get a good night's sleep and watch your general health and mental attitude

You will want a clear head at the interview. Take care of a cold or any other minor ailment, and of course, no hangovers.

What should be done on the day of the interview?

Now comes the day of the interview itself. Give yourself plenty of time to get there. Plan to arrive somewhat ahead of the scheduled time, particularly if your appointment is in the fore part of the day. If a previous candidate fails to appear, the board might be ready for you a bit early. By early afternoon an oral board is almost invariably behind schedule if there are many candidates, and you may have to wait. Take along a book or magazine to read, or your application to review, but leave any extraneous material in the waiting room when you go in for your interview. In any event, relax and compose yourself.

The matter of dress is important. The board is forming impressions about you – from your experience, your manners, your attitude, and your appearance. Give your personal appearance careful attention. Dress your best, but not your flashiest. Choose conservative, appropriate clothing, and be sure it is immaculate. This is a business interview, and your appearance should indicate that you regard it as such. Besides, being well groomed and properly dressed will help boost your confidence.

Sooner or later, someone will call your name and escort you into the interview room. *This is it.* From here on you are on your own. It is too late for any more preparation. But remember, you asked for this opportunity to prove your fitness, and you are here because your request was granted.

What happens when you go in?

The usual sequence of events will be as follows: The clerk (who is often the board stenographer) will introduce you to the chairman of the oral board, who will introduce you to the other members of the board. Acknowledge the introductions before you sit down. Do not be surprised if you find a microphone facing you or a stenotypist sitting by. Oral interviews are usually recorded in the event of an appeal or other review.

Usually the chairman of the board will open the interview by reviewing the highlights of your education and work experience from your application – primarily for the benefit of the other members of the board, as well as to get the material into the record. Do not interrupt or comment unless there is an error or significant misinterpretation; if that is the case, do not hesitate. But do not quibble about insignificant matters. Also, he will usually ask you some question about your education, experience or your present job – partly to get you to start talking and to establish the interviewing "rapport." He may start the actual questioning, or turn it over to one of the other members. Frequently, each member undertakes the questioning on a particular area, one in which he is perhaps most competent, so you can expect each member to participate in the examination. Because time is limited, you may also expect some rather abrupt switches in the direction the questioning takes, so do not be upset by it. Normally, a board member will not pursue a single line of questioning unless he discovers a particular strength or weakness.

After each member has participated, the chairman will usually ask whether any member has any further questions, then will ask you if you have anything you wish to add. Unless you are expecting this question, it may floor you. Worse, it may start you off on an extended, extemporaneous speech. The board is not usually seeking more information. The question is principally to offer you a last opportunity to present further qualifications or to indicate that you have nothing to add. So, if you feel that a significant qualification or characteristic has been overlooked, it is proper to point it out in a sentence or so. Do not compliment the board on the thoroughness of their examination – they have been sketchy, and you know it. If you wish, merely say, "No thank you, I have nothing further to add." This is a point where you can "talk yourself out" of a good impression or fail to present an important bit of information. Remember, *you close the interview yourself.*

The chairman will then say, "That is all, Mr. _____, thank you." Do not be startled; the interview is over, and quicker than you think. Thank him, gather your belongings and take your leave. Save your sigh of relief for the other side of the door.

How to put your best foot forward

Throughout this entire process, you may feel that the board individually and collectively is trying to pierce your defenses, seek out your hidden weaknesses and embarrass and confuse you. Actually, this is not true. They are obliged to make an appraisal of your qualifications for the job you are seeking, and they want to see you in your best light. Remember, they must interview all candidates and a non-cooperative candidate may become a failure in spite of their best efforts to bring out his qualifications. Here are 15 suggestions that will help you:

1) Be natural – Keep your attitude confident, not cocky

If you are not confident that you can do the job, do not expect the board to be. Do not apologize for your weaknesses, try to bring out your strong points. The board is interested in a positive, not negative, presentation. Cockiness will antagonize any board member and make him wonder if you are covering up a weakness by a false show of strength.

2) Get comfortable, but don't lounge or sprawl

Sit erectly but not stiffly. A careless posture may lead the board to conclude that you are careless in other things, or at least that you are not impressed by the importance of the occasion. Either conclusion is natural, even if incorrect. Do not fuss with your clothing, a pencil or an ashtray. Your hands may occasionally be useful to emphasize a point; do not let them become a point of distraction.

3) Do not wisecrack or make small talk

This is a serious situation, and your attitude should show that you consider it as such. Further, the time of the board is limited – they do not want to waste it, and neither should you.

4) Do not exaggerate your experience or abilities

In the first place, from information in the application or other interviews and sources, the board may know more about you than you think. Secondly, you probably will not get away with it. An experienced board is rather adept at spotting such a situation, so do not take the chance.

5) If you know a board member, do not make a point of it, yet do not hide it

Certainly you are not fooling him, and probably not the other members of the board. Do not try to take advantage of your acquaintanceship – it will probably do you little good.

6) Do not dominate the interview

Let the board do that. They will give you the clues – do not assume that you have to do all the talking. Realize that the board has a number of questions to ask you, and do not try to take up all the interview time by showing off your extensive knowledge of the answer to the first one.

7) Be attentive

You only have 20 minutes or so, and you should keep your attention at its sharpest throughout. When a member is addressing a problem or question to you, give him your undivided attention. Address your reply principally to him, but do not exclude the other board members.

8) Do not interrupt

A board member may be stating a problem for you to analyze. He will ask you a question when the time comes. Let him state the problem, and wait for the question.

9) Make sure you understand the question

Do not try to answer until you are sure what the question is. If it is not clear, restate it in your own words or ask the board member to clarify it for you. However, do not haggle about minor elements.

10) Reply promptly but not hastily

A common entry on oral board rating sheets is "candidate responded readily," or "candidate hesitated in replies." Respond as promptly and quickly as you can, but do not jump to a hasty, ill-considered answer.

11) Do not be peremptory in your answers

A brief answer is proper – but do not fire your answer back. That is a losing game from your point of view. The board member can probably ask questions much faster than you can answer them.

12) Do not try to create the answer you think the board member wants

He is interested in what kind of mind you have and how it works – not in playing games. Furthermore, he can usually spot this practice and will actually grade you down on it.

13) Do not switch sides in your reply merely to agree with a board member

Frequently, a member will take a contrary position merely to draw you out and to see if you are willing and able to defend your point of view. Do not start a debate, yet do not surrender a good position. If a position is worth taking, it is worth defending.

14) Do not be afraid to admit an error in judgment if you are shown to be wrong

The board knows that you are forced to reply without any opportunity for careful consideration. Your answer may be demonstrably wrong. If so, admit it and get on with the interview.

15) Do not dwell at length on your present job

The opening question may relate to your present assignment. Answer the question but do not go into an extended discussion. You are being examined for a *new* job, not your present one. As a matter of fact, try to phrase ALL your answers in terms of the job for which you are being examined.

Basis of Rating

Probably you will forget most of these "do's" and "don'ts" when you walk into the oral interview room. Even remembering them all will not ensure you a passing grade. Perhaps you did not have the qualifications in the first place. But remembering them will help you to put your best foot forward, without treading on the toes of the board members.

Rumor and popular opinion to the contrary notwithstanding, an oral board wants you to make the best appearance possible. They know you are under pressure – but they also want to see how you respond to it as a guide to what your reaction would be under the pressures of the job you seek. They will be influenced by the degree of poise you display, the personal traits you show and the manner in which you respond.

ABOUT THIS BOOK

This book contains tests divided into Examination Sections. Go through each test, answering every question in the margin. We have also attached a sample answer sheet at the back of the book that can be removed and used. At the end of each test look at the answer key and check your answers. On the ones you got wrong, look at the right answer choice and learn. Do not fill in the answers first. Do not memorize the questions and answers, but understand the answer and principles involved. On your test, the questions will likely be different from the samples. Questions are changed and new ones added. If you understand these past questions you should have success with any changes that arise. Tests may consist of several types of questions. We have additional books on each subject should more study be advisable or necessary for you. Finally, the more you study, the better prepared you will be. This book is intended to be the last thing you study before you walk into the examination room. Prior study of relevant texts is also recommended. NLC publishes some of these in our Fundamental Series. Knowledge and good sense are important factors in passing your exam. Good luck also helps. So now study this Passbook, absorb the material contained within and take that knowledge into the examination. Then do your best to pass that exam.

EXAMINATION SECTION

EXAMINATION SECTION
TEST 1

DIRECTIONS: Each question or incomplete statement is followed by several suggested answers or completions. Select the one that BEST answers the question or completes the statement. *PRINT THE LETTER OF THE CORRECT ANSWER IN THE SPACE AT THE RIGHT.*

1. The Federal and State grades of food are dependent upon   1.____

   A. appearance and freedom from defects
   B. maturity or freshness
   C. variety
   D. shape, color, and size
   E. color, flavor, and size

2. Select vegetables and fruits are   2.____

   A. wilted or withered
   B. ripe and well-colored
   C. picked over
   D. plump, well-colored, and ripe, firm without decay
   E. well-colored, plump, firm, and top grade

3. All perishable vegetables need to be   3.____

   A. refrigerated
   B. washed and wrapped
   C. washed, wrapped, and refrigerated
   D. stored at room temperature
   E. stored in a special compartment in the refrigerator

4. Fresh fruits, apples, pears, and peaches should be   4.____

   A. washed and wrapped separately
   B. refrigerated
   C. wrapped and stored, unwashed, in the refrigerator or other cool place
   D. kept at room temperature
   E. purchased just as they are needed

5. Dried vegetables are   5.____

   A. equal to fresh vegetables of the same variety in mineral and cellulose
   B. low-cost sources of protein and energy food
   C. good main dish foods
   D. usually cheaper than fresh vegetables
   E. all of the above

6. Commercially canned foods are   6.____

   A. economical
   B. convenient
   C. easy to store

D. available
E. important to family food supply because of economy, convenience, and availability

7. Modern frozen foods are prepared

    A. by lowering the temperature slowly to freezing
    B. by lowering the temperature of a food rapidly to freezing
    C. from average grade food products
    D. at the peak of the seasonal supply
    E. at the sacrifice of vitamins

8. To insure color retention and prevent the spoilage action of bacteria, yeasts, and molds, frozen foods should be kept at _____ degrees F.

    A. 10   B. 0   C. just under 32
    D. 20   E. 25-30

9. The grade stamp on beef, veal, calf, lamb, and mutton is one's guide to

    A. fat content
    B. leanness
    C. freedom from disease
    D. wholesomeness and quality characteristics
    E. price

10. Identity of the cuts of meat is helpful because of

    A. economy   B. method of cooking
    C. tenderness   D. all of the above
    E. none of the above

11. One will become a more economical shopper if cost of food is figured in terms of

    A. pounds
    B. quarts
    C. servings
    D. weight or measurement
    E. unit by which food is sold

12. The word poultry is applied to

    A. chickens and turkeys
    B. geese and ducks
    C. guineas and pigeons
    D. any wild bird used for food
    E. all domesticated birds used as food

13. Eggs are graded according to

    A. quality of white
    B. quality of yolk
    C. appearance of shell
    D. size
    E. size and quality of white and yolk

14. Coffee and tea contain 14.____

    A. vitamins B. nutrients C. stimulants
    D. all of the above E. none of the above

15. With higher incomes and larger food budgets, Americans are using 15.____

    A. smaller amounts of cereal products
    B. more bread
    C. less fruits and vegetables
    D. more meat and less poultry
    E. greater amounts of cereal products

16. Prepared mixes 16.____

    A. are convenient
    B. are timesaving
    C. always cost more than homemade products
    D. should be firmly packaged
    E. are convenient and timesaving, and sometimes are economical

17. The well-planned kitchen includes areas for 17.____

    A. storage B. cleanup C. preparation
    D. service E. all of the above

18. The selection of kitchen equipment considers 18.____

    A. materials
    B. construction
    C. design
    D. cost
    E. items well-constructed of durable materials in pleasing designs at reasonable costs

19. One of the MOST important things to remember about the kitchen is 19.____

    A. to keep everything immaculately clean
    B. to keep everything in its place
    C. to get as many labor-saving devices as possible
    D. to use all safety precautions - the kitchen can be a dangerous place
    E. that a great deal of the homemaker's time is spent here

20. Meal patterns vary as to 20.____

    A. cost
    B. kinds of foods
    C. amount of time and skill required for preparation
    D. all of the above
    E. none of the above

21. A distinctive menu includes 21.____

    A. flavor and texture contrast
    B. pleasing colors
    C. basic nutrients

D. family likes and dislikes
E. nutrients in pleasing flavor, texture, and color contrasts

22. The trend in modern meal service is toward

    A. very casual service
    B. traditional service
    C. more casual service with some meals served traditionally
    D. elaborate service
    E. a relaxed atmosphere with a hope that all service turns out well

22.____

23. The term flatware refers to

    A. pitchers
    B. trays and flat dishes
    C. knives, forks, and spoons
    D. anything made from stainless steel or silver
    E. teapots

23.____

24. A good design for dishes, glassware, and other service should be

    A. functional
    B. ornate
    C. simple
    D. an expression of the hostess' personality
    E. both beautiful and functional

24.____

25. The MOST practical choice for every day dinnerware for the family with several small children would be

    A. earthenware
    B. high-silicate porcelain china
    C. semi-vitrified china
    D. durable molded plastic
    E. pottery

25.____

KEY (CORRECT ANSWERS)

1.	D	11.	C
2.	D	12.	E
3.	C	13.	E
4.	C	14.	C
5.	E	15.	A
6.	E	16.	E
7.	B	17.	E
8.	B	18.	E
9.	D	19.	D
10.	D	20.	D

21. E
22. C
23. C
24. E
25. D

TEST 2

DIRECTIONS: Each question or incomplete statement is followed by several suggested answers or completions. Select the one that BEST answers the question or completes the statement. *PRINT THE LETTER OF THE CORRECT ANSWER IN THE SPACE AT THE RIGHT.*

1. The MOST suitable choice for cake and frosting combination is   1.____
    - A. angel food cake with thick buttery frosting
    - B. buttery frosting on a simple economy cake
    - C. light fluffy cooked frosting on a simple cake
    - D. angel food cake with a heavy cooked frosting
    - E. a simple chocolate cake with a chewy boiled frosting

2. Cookies   2.____
    - A. are good with most meals
    - B. can be frozen, raw, or baked
    - C. are usually inexpensive and easy to store
    - D. are easy to prepare
    - E. all of the above

3. Hot water and *stir and roll* are nonconventional methods of making   3.____
    - A. cake
    - B. cream puffs
    - C. bread
    - D. pie crust
    - E. cookies

4. Nutmeats and bits of fruit are coated with flour before mixing them into cakes or cookies to   4.____
    - A. help them sink to the bottom of the dough
    - B. keep them evenly distributed throughout the dough
    - C. keep them on top of the dough
    - D. make them more attractive
    - E. hold in their flavor

5. Poultry may be safely prepared by   5.____
    - A. stuffing and freezing it
    - B. stuffing it just before cooking
    - C. leaving the stuffing in the cooked bird for a long time
    - D. refrigerating poultry and stuffing separately two days before cooking
    - E. none of the above

6. Cooked leftover meat, poultry, or fish may be used for   6.____
    - A. casseroles
    - B. salads
    - C. sandwiches
    - D. ingredients for main dishes, salads, or sandwiches
    - E. none of the above

7. Every person who prepares or serves food should   7.____

    A. know and use ways to prevent food contamination or poisoning
    B. be especially clean and healthy
    C. keep foods very hot or very cold
    D. observe all of the above
    E. observe none of the above

8. A recent trend in entertaining with food service is   8.____

    A. buffet   B. cafeteria
    C. out-of-doors meals   D. teas
    E. coffees

9. The school lunch should be   9.____

    A. attractive, nutritious, and have variety
    B. made up of sandwiches
    C. providing half of the day"s calories
    D. packed in any sort of container
    E. given little planning time

10. Diets for the overweight are made up of   10.____

    A. foods high in calories, vitamins, and minerals
    B. foods low in calories, high in protein, vitamins, and minerals
    C. smaller servings of the regular family meals
    D. foods high in cellulose
    E. foods prepared with plenty of seasoning

11. Mental activity takes   11.____

    A. many calories   B. few calories
    C. much energy   D. more protein
    E. more fat in the diet

12. If the breadwinner works as a factory worker or farmer, he may need   12.____

    A. less food
    B. more iron
    C. more calories, perhaps as snacks
    D. more riboflavin
    E. a greater variety of food

13. In middle life, more _____ are needed to protect the body.   13.____

    A. fruits   B. vegetables
    C. calories   D. proteins
    E. fruits and vegetables

14. Older people need decreased numbers of calories and increased amounts of protein,   14.____
    vitamins, and minerals because

    A. the metabolic rate has slowed
    B. they are not so active
    C. their incomes are less

7

D. shopping for food is more difficult
E. their bodies are less active and the metabolic rate is slowed

15. It is wise to divide foods fairly evenly among three meals a day for

    A. older people
    B. middle-aged people
    C. teenagers
    D. children
    E. all ages

16. Consideration and thoughtfulness is the MOST important part of

    A. adjusting to special diets
    B. reactions to income increases
    C. reactions to income losses
    D. appreciation of unusual foods
    E. learning to cook

17. The healthier a child is between the years of six and twelve,

    A. the better adult health he will have
    B. the better teeth he will have
    C. the taller he will grow
    D. the better adjustments he will make in adolescence
    E. will not affect his future health

18. Pre-adolescent children need

    A. extra calcium and protein for growth
    B. iodine to help regulate the use of food
    C. quick-acting foods for extra energy
    D. minerals and vitamins for body regulation, protein for growth, and extra foods for quick energy
    E. starches and extras between meals

19. One of the MOST important events in the daily dietary life of each family member is

    A. breakfast
    B. lunch
    C. dinner or supper
    D. snack time
    E. the coffee break

20. It is good to remember to give a small child

    A. large servings
    B. small servings with seconds if he desires
    C. a wide variety of foods at the same meal
    D. several foods which are new to him
    E. food which he must eat

21. Children enjoy

    A. highly spiced foods
    B. very cold foods
    C. rough textures
    D. very hot foods
    E. warm foods of smooth texture and mild flavor

22. An infant should be fed 22.____
    A. in a relaxed atmosphere
    B. when he is hungry
    C. with a balanced diet
    D. on a definite schedule
    E. in a relaxed way, a balanced diet when he is hungry

23. When meat and low-acid vegetables are canned, it is necessary to use a temperature of 23.____
    _____ to kill bacteria.

    A. 100° F   B. 144° F
    C. 200° F   D. 400° F
    E. higher than boiling

24. Foods satisfactorily preserved by a concentration of sugar are 24.____
    A. meats
    B. fruits
    C. vegetables
    D. fruits and some vegetables
    E. whole fruits, or fruit and vegetable juices

25. It may be necessary to add _____ to fruit pulp or juice to make jelly. 25.____
    A. commercial pectin
    B. apple juice
    C. gelatin
    D. alcohol
    E. commercial pectin or apple juice

26. Good food packaging for freezing 26.____
    A. prevents freezer *burn*
    B. prevents transfer of flavor
    C. prevents transfer of odor
    D. need not be leakproof
    E. prevents loss of flavor, odor, color, and moisture

27. Scalding of vegetables before freezing helps 27.____
    A. retain color
    B. retard enzyme growth
    C. destroys some bacteria
    D. may soften and shrink the vegetables
    E. to do all of the above

28. Overscalding of vegetables before freezing 28.____
    A. causes an increase of sugar
    B. absorbs food values soluble in hot water
    C. destroys vitamins
    D. makes the product too soft
    E. does no harm

29. Darkening of color from enzyme action will take place in _____ unless ascorbic acid is used.

    A. vegetables
    B. fruits
    C. peaches, apples, and pears
    D. tomatoes
    E. meat

30. Before freezing, remove excess _____ from meat, fish, or poultry.

    A. fat
    B. bone
    C. skin
    D. membranes
    E. materials which will become rancid or waste space

KEY (CORRECT ANSWERS)

1. B	11. B	21. E
2. E	12. C	22. E
3. D	13. E	23. E
4. B	14. E	24. D
5. B	15. E	25. E
6. D	16. A	26. E
7. D	17. A	27. E
8. C	18. D	28. B
9. A	19. A	29. C
10. B	20. B	30. E

TEST 3

DIRECTIONS: Each question or incomplete statement is followed by several suggested answers or completions. Select the one that BEST answers the question or completes the statement. *PRINT THE LETTER OF THE CORRECT ANSWER IN THE SPACE AT THE RIGHT.*

1. Americans became nutrition-conscious approximately seventy years ago with the isolation of   1.____

    A. carbohydrates B. fats C. proteins
    D. minerals E. vitamins

2. A family food plan should include   2.____

    A. sufficient foods from each basic group
    B. choices which meet all the likes of the family
    C. carbohydrates which are less expensive
    D. an abundance of protein
    E. foods containing delicious fats

3. A food plan made a week in advance   3.____

    A. allows one to shop ahead
    B. makes certain that all nutrients will be included
    C. shows how family needs will be met, amount of food needed, and something of cost
    D. is time consuming
    E. allows one to buy foods at bargain prices

4. A simplified food selection guide for healthful living builds meals around   4.____

    A. dairy foods B. meats
    C. breads and cereals D. vegetables and fruits
    E. all of the above

5. If thought is used in the family menu planning, an adequate supply of protein at a *low* cost may be secured from   5.____

    A. beef and veal
    B. pork and lamb
    C. poultry and fish
    D. dry beans, peas, and nuts
    E. meats and protein substitutes

6. Teenagers, pregnant women, and nursing mothers need LARGER amounts of _____ than do other family members.   6.____

    A. dairy foods B. fruits and vegetables
    C. meats D. breads and cereals
    E. all of the above

7. _____ servings of fruits and vegetables, and, breads and cereals should be included for adequate food intake.   7.____

A.	Two	B.	Three	C.	One
D.	Five	E.	At least four or more		

8. Research studies show the diets of teenagers are *likely* to be   8.___

   A. well-balanced
   B. poorly balanced
   C. lacking in protein and vitamins and minerals
   D. high in vitamins and minerals
   E. adequate in fruits and vegetables

9. When the daily caloric requirement is exceeded, that not used is   9.___

   A. excreted as waste
   B. stored as muscle protein
   C. stored as fat
   D. used for energy
   E. used for heat

10. The MAIN job of _____ is to build and repair body tissue.   10.___

    A. carbohydrates   B. proteins   C. minerals
    D. vitamins   E. fats

11. A unit used to measure the warmth and energy value of a food is the   11.___

    A. amino acid   B. calorie   C. kilogram
    D. ounce   E. atom

12. Individual caloric requirements depend upon   12.___

    A. age and sex
    B. temperature and kind of food eaten
    C. type and amount of exercise
    D. proportion of one's nonfat body weight
    E. all of the above

13. _____ creates bulk which helps to keep the digestive tract working smoothly.   13.___

    A. Water   B. Cellulose
    C. Protein   D. Fat
    E. Carbohydrate

14. _____ cups of liquid should be included in the daily food intake to promote body regulation and elimination.   14.___

    A. Four   B. Five   C. Six   D. Seven   E. Eight

15. Good nutrition requires that one be able to   15.___

    A. discriminate between fact and fallacy in fad diets of today
    B. spend money for *health foods* and *health aids*
    C. purchase highly advertised brands of foods
    D. all of the above
    E. none of the above

16. One's nutritional health depends not only on the selection of a balanced diet but upon   16.____

    A. how this food has been stored before its use
    B. how it has been prepared
    C. how the body is able to use the nutrients
    D. all of the above
    E. none of the above

17. The MOST important factor in development of malnutrition is   17.____

    A. lack of sleep
    B. too little fresh air and sunshine
    C. fatigue
    D. faulty diet
    E. pressure of social life

18. The FIRST step in a weight-control project is to   18.____

    A. begin a program of strenuous exercise
    B. go on a diet to lose or gain weight
    C. try special diets advertised
    D. go on as one has been doing
    E. have a physical check-up by a doctor

19. Food requires a larger portion of the family income than any other item, using _____   19.____
    percent of the income varying with the amount of income.

    A. 25-50   B. 50-75   C. 33   D. 20   E. 60

20. It is possible to have a nutritionally adequate diet on less money than the average family   20.____
    spends by

    A. gaining more knowledge about nutrition
    B. considering more economical shopping procedures
    C. developing an interest in nutrition, consumer practices, and food habits
    D. changing food habits
    E. altering food habits and buying habits after studying nutrition

21. Good food management is essential to   21.____

    A. help economize while replenishing stored food supplies
    B. alter *expensive* food tastes
    C. develop greater numbers of food likes and fewer dislikes
    D. control meals eaten away from home
    E. meet the rise in the cost of staple goods

22. When one shops for food, it is wise to   22.____

    A. compare the market order with the Basic Four
    B. compare food prices and quality
    C. figure the food budget closely in advance
    D. be a careful, ethical shopper
    E. shop carefully and wisely with a good market order which was made considering the Basic Four, prices, and quality

23. State and Federal laws protect consumers from adulterated foods including   23.____

    A. food that may be injurious to health or in such condition as to be unfit for human food
    B. food that has been packed, packaged, or stored under unsanitary conditions
    C. food that uses coal-tar dyes
    D. food that is falsely labeled or has substitutes
    E. foods or any ingredients that use harmful colors or substitutes, or that may be prepared or stored in unsanitary ways so as to injure humans

24. The Federal Food and Drug Act, created in 1906, helps to safeguard our food supply by   24.____

    A. prohibiting false advertising of food, drugs, and cosmetics
    B. requiring the package label to give weight, measure, and contents
    C. prohibiting the transportation in interstate commerce of adulterated or misbranded foods
    D. all of the above
    E. none of the above

25. The MOST important factors in buying food are   25.____

    A. quality and price
    B. price and convenience
    C. quality and convenience
    D. quality, price, and convenience
    E. price and services available

KEY (CORRECT ANSWERS)

1.	E	11.	B
2.	A	12.	E
3.	C	13.	B
4.	E	14.	E
5.	E	15.	A
6.	A	16.	D
7.	E	17.	D
8.	C	18.	E
9.	C	19.	A
10.	B	20.	E

21. E
22. E
23. E
24. D
25. D

TEST 4

DIRECTIONS: Each question or incomplete statement is followed by several suggested answers or completions. Select the one that BEST answers the question or completes the statement. *PRINT THE LETTER OF THE CORRECT ANSWER IN THE SPACE AT THE RIGHT.*

1. Centerpieces

    A. require little time and thought to arrange attractively
    B. using very fragrant flowers are good
    C. are expensive
    D. made by careful application of design principles are best
    E. should be high

2. A convenient way to serve many people with the MINIMUM amount of assistance and space is _____ service.

    A. compromise   B. plate   C. American
    D. formal   E. buffet

3. For the family type meal service, all food is passed

    A. to the left
    B. to the right
    C. either right or left as the family decides
    D. the direction which gives the shortest distance
    E. as the hostess indicates

4. The person served FIRST at dinner is *usually* the

    A. hostess
    B. host
    C. gentleman guest
    D. person seated at the right of the host
    E. person seated at the right of the hostess

5. Cookery can be fascinating allowing for

    A. creativity
    B. observation
    C. concentration
    D. management skill
    E. keen observation, concentrated management, and unlimited creativity

6. To use recipes effectively, it is necessary to

    A. understand terms and measurements
    B. use standard measuring tools
    C. have a knowledge of how substitutions may be made
    D. use correct ingredient combinations
    E. all of the above

7. To prevent excessive shrinkage of meat, use _____ roasting temperatures.   7._____

   A. very low - below 275° F
   B. slow - about 325° F
   C. moderate - 350° F
   D. hot - 400° F
   E. very hot - 450° F

8. In conventional cooking, heat is applied to the surface of the food, but by electronic cook-   8._____
   ing the food is cooked

   A. by energy
   B. by agitation of molecules
   C. by absorption of microwave energy and the resulting heat
   D. a golden brown
   E. a long time

9. Seasonings are used to _____ natural flavors in foods.   9._____

   A. hide   B. overpower
   C. bring out   D. alter
   E. disguise unpleasant

10. All oven temperatures in recipes are   10._____

    A. set when the product is put in the oven
    B. preheated temperatures
    C. set after the product is mixed
    D. approximate temperatures
    E. double-checked by use of a separate oven thermometer

11. Extra time is allowed in addition to time for meat cookery to   11._____

    A. allow the meat to set
    B. make the gravy
    C. carve the meat
    D. make carving easier and prepare gravy
    E. be certain the meat is cooked

12. Eggs and cheese should be cooked at _____ temperatures.   12._____

    A. very high   B. high
    C. moderate   D. low to moderate
    E. very low

13. To cook vegetables BEST,   13._____

    A. use little water and cook quickly
    B. cook slowly
    C. use a generous amount of water
    D. pare generously
    E. pour off cooking liquid

14. For BEST results, cook frozen vegetables

    A. as you would fresh vegetables
    B. the same as fresh vegetables, but reduce the cooking time
    C. in a pressure pan
    D. after thawing completely
    E. in a cup of water

15. Fruit cooked in sugar syrup

    A. retains its natural raw flavor
    B. loses its shape
    C. loses its vitamin content
    D. does keep its shape, but has a changed flavor
    E. remains unchanged in shape or flavor

16. All-purpose flour is

    A. a blend of hard and soft wheat flours
    B. not desirable for pastries
    C. whole wheat flour
    D. enriched with gluten
    E. more expensive than other flour

17. The _____ in wheat flour makes it possible to develop an elastic dough from it.

    A. bran   B. germ   C. vitamin B   D. starch   E. gluten

18. Points to consider when evaluating commercial or homemade mixes with conventional mixing methods are

    A. cost
    B. time involved
    C. quality of resulting product
    D. convenience
    E. analyses of the quality of final products by cost, time, and convenience

19. Essentials for making a good cup of coffee or tea are

    A. fresh ingredients
    B. freshly cleaned containers
    C. plenty of beverage to be reheated
    D. good fresh coffee or tea, a clean container, and water of the correct temperature
    E. dated ingredients

20. The BEST time to satisfy the craving for sweets is

    A. with a dessert at mealtime
    B. by eating candy between meals
    C. by eating desserts between meals as snacks
    D. by eating candy just after a meal
    E. whenever the craving arises

21. To adjust a cake recipe for higher altitudes, it may be necessary to   21.____

    A. increase leavening and sugar
    B. decrease leavening or sugar or both
    C. increase liquid
    D. decrease leavening or sugar and increase liquid
    E. increase the shortening

22. Butter cakes are USUALLY made by the _____ methods.   22.____

    A. conventional   B. one bowl quick
    C. sponge   D. conventional or quick
    E. none of the above

23. The characteristics of good plain pastry are   23.____

    A. light, crisp, tender, flaky crust and golden brown color
    B. firm, smooth golden crust
    C. a tender crumbling crust
    D. shrunken edges
    E. a very pale crust

24. The temperature at which candy is cooked determines   24.____

    A. the texture
    B. the softness
    C. the hardness or brittleness
    D. the desired consistency
    E. flavor

25. The amount of handling candy receives after cooking determines   25.____

    A. the flavor
    B. the texture - crystalline or noncrystalline
    C. hardness
    D. softness
    E. texture and consistency

KEY (CORRECT ANSWERS)

1. D
2. E
3. B
4. D
5. E

6. E
7. B
8. C
9. C
10. B

11. D
12. D
13. A
14. B
15. D

16. A
17. E
18. E
19. D
20. A

21. D
22. D
23. A
24. D
25. B

EXAMINATION SECTION
TEST 1

DIRECTIONS: Each question or incomplete statement is followed by several suggested answers or completions. Select the one that BEST answers the question or completes the statement. *PRINT THE LETTER OF THE CORRECT ANSWER IN THE SPACE AT THE RIGHT.*

1. Which of the following fats has the HIGHEST smoking temperature?   1.____
   - A. Butter
   - B. Soybean oil
   - C. Hydrogenated oil
   - D. Olive oil

2. The smoke which is given off from heated fats when they begin to decompose contains   2.____
   - A. glycerol
   - B. sterol
   - C. acrolein
   - D. stearin

3. Fat in a recipe is called *shortening* because it shortens the   3.____
   - A. time of preparation
   - B. time for baking
   - C. gluten strands
   - D. sugar particles

4. The irritating gas that is produced by overheating fat is called   4.____
   - A. sterol
   - B. palmitate
   - C. glycerol
   - D. acrolein

5. The LESS saturated animal fats are found in   5.____
   - A. poultry and pork
   - B. fish
   - C. beef
   - D. lamb

6. High in unsaturated fat content is   6.____
   - A. coconut oil
   - B. soybean oil
   - C. tallow
   - D. butter

7. One cup of margarine weighs APPROXIMATELY _____ pound.   7.____
   - A. 1/2
   - B. 1
   - C. 3/4
   - D. 1/4

8. MOST of the volatile oils that give flavors to spices and herbs will have disappeared by the time they have been stored for a period of about   8.____
   - A. six weeks
   - B. six months
   - C. twelve months
   - D. eighteen months

9. Mayonnaise should be stored   9.____
   - A. in the coldest part of the refrigerator
   - B. in the freezer
   - C. on the closet shelf
   - D. in the refrigerator away from the coldest part

10. Fat which contributes to tenderness in meats is called _____ fat.   10.____
    - A. unsaturated
    - B. protective
    - C. marbling
    - D. saturated

11. One pound of hydrogenated shortening will measure to be _____ cup(s).

    A. 1   B. 1 1/2   C. 2   D. 2 1/2

12. One pound of dried eggs is APPROXIMATELY equivalent to _____ eggs.

    A. 15-18   B. 30-40   C. 20-25   D. 50-60

13. Federal law regulates foods sold in

    A. cities
    C. states
    B. rural areas
    D. interstate commerce

14. When storing eggs at home, _____ refrigerator.

    A. store in original container outside
    B. wash and place in an open bowl in the
    C. do not wash and leave in original container in
    D. place, unwashed, in an open dish in the

15. The average weight of a large egg is _____ ounce(s).

    A. 1   B. 4   C. 2   D. 3

16. The green discoloration noticed on the bottom of omelets and around the yolks of hard-cooked eggs is caused by the formation of

    A. ferrous sulfide
    C. sulfurous avidin
    B. ferric caseinate
    D. sulfur dioxide

17. To know the quality of eggs, look for the label stamped on the carton

    A. *selected*
    C. *best*
    B. *grade A*
    D. *fresh country eggs*

18. The freshness of an egg is recognized by

    A. color of the yolk
    B. relative quantity of yolk and albumin
    C. relative size of air space within shell
    D. color of the shell

19. An INCORRECT statement about eggs is:

    A. The food value of grade A is greater than that of grade C
    B. It is illegal to sell ungraded eggs in New York
    C. The color of the shell has nothing to do with grade
    D. Blood spots are not harmful

20. Freshness in an opened egg can be recognized by the fact that the

    A. yolk breaks easily
    B. white spreads and seems watery
    C. yolk has a pale color
    D. yolk stands firm and high

21. According to U.S.D.A. requirements, a dozen large eggs must weigh _____ ounces. 21._____
    A. 24   B. 18   C. 30   D. 36

22. For short-time storage, eggs keep BEST at 22._____
    A. 30° F   B. 45° F   C. 65° F   D. 72° F

23. More than half of the beef on the United States market bears the grade U.S. 23._____
    A. 1A Prime   B. 3 Medium   C. Choice   D. 2 Good

24. In aging meat, sides of beef are stored at room temperature in order to 24._____
    A. tenderize
    B. develop flavor
    C. reduce strong flavor
    D. sterilize

25. Mutton is obtained from 25._____
    A. lamb   B. hog   C. sheep   D. calf

KEY (CORRECT ANSWERS)

1. C
2. D
3. C
4. D
5. B

6. B
7. A
8. B
9. D
10. C

11. D
12. B
13. D
14. C
15. D

16. A
17. B
18. C
19. A
20. D

21. A
22. B
23. D
24. A
25. C

TEST 2

DIRECTIONS: Each question or incomplete statement is followed by several suggested answers or completions. Select the one that BEST answers the question or completes the statement. *PRINT THE LETTER OF THE CORRECT ANSWER IN THE SPACE AT THE RIGHT.*

1. Frozen meat is BEST preserved when maintained

   A. in moisture-proof material at 0° F
   B. in cheesecloth at 0° F
   C. unwrapped at 0° F
   D. unwrapped at -20° F

1.____

2. Compared with grain-fed beef, forage-fed beef is

   A. inferior in vitamin A value
   B. richer in vitamin A
   C. higher in fat content
   D. more tender

2.____

3. The government stamp on meats indicates _____ meat.

   A. poor   B. tender
   C. wholesome   D. expensive

3.____

4. Toughness of meat is MAINLY due to

   A. the fat distributed within it
   B. the presence of bones
   C. the presence of connective tissue
   D. its muscle fiber arrangement

4.____

5. For the medium degree of doneness of meat, the internal temperature should be between _____° F.

   A. 122-140   B. 135-140   C. 158-165   D. 140-160

5.____

6. Chipped or dried beef is made from

   A. cured rounds of low-grade beef
   B. cured picnic shoulders
   C. corned beef
   D. salt pork

6.____

7. Cured boned pork loin is called

   A. Canadian style bacon   B. Virginia ham
   C. country ham   D. Boston butt

7.____

8. Variety meats are

   A. game meats   B. specially cut roasts
   C. organs of animals   D. pickled and smoked meats

8.____

9. Variety meats are NOT commonly used in family meals because

    A. they are difficult to digest
    B. they are expensive
    C. people have predetermined ideas about them
    D. butchers do not have them

10. Grading of meat is

    A. compulsory by law throughout the United States
    B. required in diet feeding
    C. based on definite characteristics of finish conformation and quality
    D. an indication of wholesomeness of meat

11. The round purple stamp on government graded meat indicates meat that is

    A. unfit for human consumption
    B. superior in quality
    C. inferior in quality
    D. fit for human consumption

12. Aging of freshly picked corn and green peas changes the flavor because of the

    A. loss of moisture
    B. loss of vitamin content
    C. conversion of some of the starch to sugar
    D. increase in yeast development

13. Deterioration of dried vegetables is retarded by

    A. marinating before drying
    B. storage in metal boxes
    C. precooking before drying
    D. infrared light treatment before packaging

14. If peeled vegetables are soaked in cold water for two hours,

    A. nutrients are lost
    B. cooking time is decreased
    C. appearance of the cooked vegetables is improved
    D. the cooked vegetable retains its form

15. Root vegetables are BEST stored in

    A. atmosphere that is maintained at 36° F
    B. dehumidified
    C. at 30° F
    D. at 75% humidity

16. Yellow turnips and white turnips furnish

    A. the same food values
    B. vitamin G
    C. carotene
    D. complete proteins

17. Potatoes which have been stored for 6 months or more

    A. have a higher sugar content than new potatoes
    B. are unsuited for potato chips
    C. have a higher starch content than new potatoes
    D. are soggy when baked

18. Red vegetables keep their color BEST if they are cooked in the presence of

    A. acid
    B. alkali
    C. steam pressure
    D. baking soda

19. Of the following, the plant which is NOT suitable as a salad green is

    A. endive
    B. watercress
    C. romaine
    D. avocado

20. Horseradish is the

    A. ground stem of the paw-paw
    B. fermented and sterilized soybean fiber
    C. ground root of a mustard-like herb
    D. fibrous stem of the horn wort

21. Before being cooked, broccoli should be soaked in salted water to

    A. remove insects
    B. improve flavor
    C. soften the texture of the stems
    D. brighten the color

22. When chemical nitrogen is added to the soil, the

    A. protein content of plants tends to be increased
    B. percentage of phosphorus, calcium, and potassium in crops is often decreased
    C. vitamin C content of oranges is sharply increased
    D. size, color, palatability, and appearance of a crop is not affected

23. A grade of meat which is good quality for all uses is

    A. prime   B. choice   C. good   D. commercial

24. Rock Cornish game hens usually weigh about _____ pound(s).

    A. 1   B. 3   C. 6-8   D. 10-15

25. One pound of dried eggs is the equivalent of about _____ eggs.

    A. 25-30   B. 35-40   C. 18-20   D. 50-60

KEY (CORRECT ANSWERS)

1. A
2. B
3. C
4. C
5. C

6. A
7. A
8. C
9. C
10. C

11. D
12. C
13. C
14. A
15. A

16. A
17. A
18. A
19. D
20. C

21. A
22. A
23. C
24. A
25. B

TEST 3

DIRECTIONS: Each question or incomplete statement is followed by several suggested answers or completions. Select the one that BEST answers the question or completes the statement. *PRINT THE LETTER OF THE CORRECT ANSWER IN THE SPACE AT THE RIGHT.*

1. The sweetening power of syrups listed according to sweetness is   1.___

    A. honey, maple, sorghum, corn syrup
    B. maple, sorghum, honey, corn syrup
    C. corn syrup, honey, maple, sorghum
    D. maple, honey, corn syrup, sorghum

2. Tapioca is a starch product prepared from   2.___

    A. the acid hydrolysis of sucrose
    B. a root of the cassava tree
    C. the hydrolysis of cornstarch
    D. a plant native to the United States

3. The inversion or splitting of cane sugar in water is hastened by   3.___

    A. the addition of maltose
    B. addition of tartaric acid
    C. no addition and heating
    D. stirring

4. Cerelose is   4.___

    A. a natural sugar   B. not a sugar
    C. natural dextrose   D. commercial dextrose

5. Which of the following is NOT a monosaccharide?   5.___

    A. Glucose   B. Maltose   C. Fructose   D. Galactose

6. The proportion of sugar used in ice cream is high because   6.___

    A. we like ice cream sweet
    B. cold diminishes the sense of sweetness
    C. it makes freezing easier
    D. it makes the cream keep better

7. A non-nutritive artificial sweetner used in ice cream is   7.___

    A. dextrin   B. nutrasweet
    C. levulose   D. maltose

8. The mineral content of brown sugar as compared with that of refined sugar is   8.___

    A. much lower   B. much higher
    C. slightly lower   D. slightly higher

9. All of the following are simple sugars EXCEPT   9.___

    A. dextrose   B. fructose   C. glucose   D. lactose

10. The solution which is used to test for the presence of sugar is

    A. Dakin's B. Fehling's
    C. Lugol's D. nitric acid

11. Sugar added to stiffly beaten egg whites produces

    A. custard B. glace C. junket D. meringue

12. The breed of cow which gives the GREATEST volume of milk but the LOWEST percentage of fat and protein is

    A. Holstein B. Jersey
    C. Guernsey D. Dutch-belted

13. Homogenized milk has been treated to

    A. remove harmful bacteria
    B. lower water content
    C. increase vitamin D content
    D. distribute fat particles evenly

14. The process that reduces the size of fat particles in milk and distributes them evenly is

    A. emulsification B. homogenization
    C. hydration D. hydrogenation

15. Pasteurized milk is preferable to raw milk because it

    A. is homogenized
    B. has minimum butter fat content
    C. is safer
    D. tastes better

16. Cheese originates in

    A. pasteurization B. fermentation
    C. inversion D. coagulation

17. Milk should be stored at a temperature not above

    A. 40° F B. 50° F C. 32° F D. 35° F

18. The *almost perfect food*, milk, furnishes a very meager supply of

    A. calcium B. niacin C. phosphorus D. iron

19. Milk which has two percent butterfat in it should be labeled

    A. buttermilk B. dry skim milk
    C. skimmed milk D. half and half

20. The following is a skim-milk cheese:

    A. Camembert B. Cheddar
    C. Parmesan D. Fromage de Brie

21. A skim milk cheese is

    A. parmesan
    B. cheddar
    C. fromage de brie
    D. camembert

22. Boiled milk cannot be used for preparing junket because boiling

    A. coagulates casein
    B. makes the calcium salts insoluble
    C. kills the lactic acid bacteria
    D. decreases the amount of important lactose

23. Milk, when placed in the refrigerator, should NOT be placed in the freezing unit but should be kept on the shelf that is

    A. lowest
    B. most accessible
    C. coolest
    D. highest

24. In naking white sauce,

    A. melt the butter, add flour, then add milk
    B. add butter to hot milk, then add dry flour
    C. mix the flour with hot milk, then add butter
    D. combine fat, flour, and milk simultaneously

25. A piece of chuck beef is MOST palatable when

    A. broiled   B. singed   C. steeped   D. braised

KEY (CORRECT ANSWERS)

1. A		11. D	
2. B		12. A	
3. B		13. D	
4. B		14. B	
5. B		15. C	
6. B		16. B	
7. B		17. B	
8. D		18. D	
9. D		19. C	
10. B		20. C	

21. A
22. B
23. C
24. A
25. D

EXAMINATION SECTION
TEST 1

DIRECTIONS: Each question or incomplete statement is followed by several suggested answers or completions. Select the one that BEST answers the question or completes the statement. *PRINT THE LETTER OF THE CORRECT ANSWER IN THE SPACE AT THE RIGHT.*

1. In food service operations, the supervisor usually can arrive at a decision concerning an operations problem by considering the following steps to a solution:
    I. Analysis of available information
    II. Definition of problem
    III. Development of alternate solutions
    IV. Selection of decision
   In which of the following options are the steps given in PROPER sequence?

   A. II, I, III, IV
   B. I, III, II, IV
   C. I, II, III, IV
   D. III, I, II, IV

   1._____

2. The one of the following which is MOST important for improvement of the productivity of food-service employees is the

   A. use of convenience foods
   B. posting of food preparation schedules for employees
   C. adoption and implementation of a program of task analysis and work measurement
   D. advance preparation of as much food as possible

   2._____

3. Assume that all of the following problems are occurring in a kitchen under your supervision: production is slow in terms of food preparation; housekeeping is lax; the quality of the food prepared is very poor; morale is low.
   Of these four problems, the one that is *most likely* the cause of all the others and should probably be attended to FIRST is

   A. slow production
   B. lax housekeeping
   C. poorly prepared food
   D. low morale

   3._____

4. A common problem in food-service supervision is that improper supervisory practices can lead to situations in which subordinates disobey direct orders given to them by their superior.
   Which of the following supervisors would be *most likely* to promote such a situation? A supervisor who

   A. does not delegate authority
   B. does not make a decision without consulting his or her entire staff
   C. is unwilling to punish any employee for an infraction of the rules
   D. rarely holds meetings with his or her staff

   4._____

5. While reviewing kitchen operations, you notice that a recently-hired employee is using too large a scoop for serving mashed potatoes. Since you personally instructed this individual in the proper utilization of serving utensils, you believe that this employee should be reprimanded.
   In this situation, the *most appropriate* of the following actions would be to

   5._____

A. call the employee aside, inform him of his mistake, and plan for additional instruction
B. inform the employee of his mistake in the presence of the other employees
C. remove the employee from his work station and assign him to some less desirable tasks
D. assign another employee to serve the mashed potatoes with the appropriate size scoop and have the recently-hired employee observe

6. Assume that you are approached individually by two employees who work together in food preparation. Each employee registers her complaint against working with the other. Which one of the following would be the MOST effective action to take in order to handle this problem?

    A. At the next regularly scheduled staff meeting, mention the importance of good working relationships.
    B. Ask your superior to make a judgment in this case, instead of deciding what to do yourself.
    C. Reassign one employee to a suitable job where she will not have to work with the other employee.
    D. Write a report to your superior detailing the problem and requesting transfers for both of the employees.

7. Suppose that, as a supervisor, you have an idea for changing the way a certain task is performed by your staff so that it will be less tedious and get done faster.
   Of the following, the MOST advisable action for you to take regarding this idea is to

    A. issue a written memorandum, explaining the new method and giving reasons why it is to replace the old one
    B. discuss it with your staff to get their reactions and suggestions
    C. set up a training class in the new method for your staff
    D. try it out on an experimental basis on half the staff

8. In preparing work schedules for food-service employees, the one of the following considerations to which the supervisor should give LEAST priority is the

    A. work skills of the employees
    B. jobs to be done
    C. physical set-up of the work area and equipment available
    D. preferences of the employees

9. A new employee complains to you that she thinks the current method of serving meals is very ineffective. This employee strongly insists that another method is much better. However, the suggested method had been tried in the past with very unsatisfactory results. Of the following, the BEST way for you to handle the situation would be to

    A. assign the employee to a different work area to avoid conflict
    B. try out the suggested method for one or two days to demonstrate why it doesn't work
    C. briefly tell the employee that her suggested method will not work
    D. discuss with the employee the reasons why the present method has proven to be more successful than her suggested method

10. Assume that you find it necessary to discipline two subordinates, Mr. Tate and Mr. Sawyer, for coming to work late on several occasions. Their latenesses have had disruptive effects on the work schedule, and you have given both of them several verbal warnings. Mr. Tate has been in your work unit for many years, and his work has always been satisfactory. Mr. Sawyer is a probationary employee who has had some problems in learning your procedures. You decide to give Mr. Tate one more warning, in private, for his latenesses.
    According to good supervisory practice, which one of the following disciplinary actions should you take with regard to Mr. Sawyer?

    A. Give him a reprimand in front of his co-workers to make a lasting impression.
    B. Recommend dismissal since he has not yet completed his probationary period.
    C. Give him one more warning, in private, for his latenesses.
    D. Recommend a short suspension or payroll deduction to impress on him the importance of coming to work on time.

11. Assume that you have delegated a very important work assignment to Johnson, one of your most experienced subordinates. Prior to completion of the assignment, your superior accidentally discovers that the assignment is being carried out incorrectly and tells you about it.
    Which one of the following responses is *most appropriate* for you to give to your superior?

    A. "I take full responsibility, and I will see to it that the assignment is carried out correctly."
    B. "Johnson has been with us for many years now and should know better."
    C. "It really isn't Johnson's fault, rather it is the fault of the ancient equipment we have to do the job."
    D. "I think you should inform Johnson since he is the one at fault, not I."

12. Assume that you observe that one of your employees is talking excessively with other employees, quitting early and taking unusually long rest periods. Despite these abuses, she is one of your most productive employees, and her work is usually of the highest quality.
    Of the following, the *most appropriate* action to take with regard to this employee is to

    A. ignore these infractions since she is one of your best workers
    B. ask your superior to reprimand her so that you can remain on the employee's good side
    C. reprimand her since not doing so would lower the morale of the other employees
    D. ask another of your subordinates to mention these infractions to the offending employee and suggest that she stop breaking rules

13. Assume that you have noticed that an employee whose attendance had been quite satisfactory is now showing marked evidence of a consistent pattern of absences.
    Of the following, the BEST way to cope with this problem is to

    A. wait several weeks to see whether this pattern continues
    B. meet with the employee to try to find out the reasons for this change
    C. call a staff meeting and discuss the need for good attendance
    D. write a carefully worded warning to the employee

14. It is generally agreed that the successful supervisor must know how to wisely delegate work to her subordinates since she cannot do everything herself.
Which one of the following practices is *most likely* to result in INEFFECTIVE delegation by a supervisor?

    A. Establishment of broad controls to assure feedback about any deviations from plans
    B. Willingness to let subordinates use their own ideas about how to get the job done, where appropriate
    C. Constant observance of employees to see if they are making any mistakes
    D. Granting of enough authority to make possible the accomplishment of the delegated work

15. Suppose that, in accordance with grievance procedures, an employee brings a complaint to you, his immediate supervisor.
In dealing with his complaint, the one of the following which is MOST important for you to do is to

    A. talk to the employee's co-workers to learn whether the complaint is justified
    B. calm the employee by assuring him that you will look into the matter as soon as possible
    C. tell your immediate superior about the employee's complaint
    D. give the employee an opportunity to tell the full story

16. The successful application by a supervisor of work simplification techniques to food preparation and service work is *most likely* to result in which one of the following?

    A. Employees working harder than before
    B. Food products of higher nutritional value
    C. Better employee attendance
    D. Elimination of unnecessary parts of jobs

17. Holding staff meetings at regular intervals is generally considered to be a good supervisory practice.
Which one of the following subjects is LEAST desirable for discussion at such a meeting?

    A. Revisions in agency personnel policies
    B. Violation of an agency rule by one of the employees present
    C. Problems of waste and breakage in the work area
    D. Complaints of employees about working conditions

18. Suppose that you are informed that your staff is soon to be reduced by one-third due to budget problems.
Which one of the following steps would be LEAST advisable in your effort to maintain a quality service with the smaller number of employees?

    A. Directing employees to speed up operations
    B. Giving employees training or retraining
    C. Rearranging the work area
    D. Revising work methods

19. Of the following, which action on the part of the supervisor is LEAST likely to contribute to upgrading the skills of her subordinates?

    A. Providing appropriate training to subordinates
    B. Making periodic evaluations of subordinates and discussing the evaluations with the subordinates
    C. Consistently assigning subordinates to those tasks with which they are familiar
    D. Giving increased responsibility to appropriate subordinates

    19._____

20. Suppose that a new employee on your staff has difficulty in performing his assigned tasks, after having been given training.
    Of the following courses of action, the one which would be BEST for you, his supervisor, to take FIRST is to

    A. change his work assignment
    B. give him a poor evaluation since he is obviously unable to do the work
    C. give him the training again
    D. have him work with an employee who is more experienced in the tasks for a short while

    20._____

21. To insure the safety of employees who must retrieve items from a food storeroom, the supervisor should direct that

    A. bulky items be put on the floor near the storeroom door
    B. newly-received items be put on the shelves in front of previously-received items
    C. ladders or step-stools be used to reach upper shelves
    D. frequently-requisitioned items be piled up just outside the entrance to the storeroom

    21._____

22. Suppose that a cook receives a minor burn, which causes a blister on his hand, while handling a hot pan of food. After seeing that the employee gets proper treatment for the burn, the MOST advisable of the following actions for the supervisor to take is to

    A. send the employee home
    B. tell the employee to return to his work station
    C. help the employee to finish the day's food preparation
    D. temporarily assign the employee to a task other than handling food

    22._____

23. Of the following, the FIRST step which should be taken by you, the supervisor, in the orientation of a new food-service employee is to

    A. include the new employee in the next regularly-scheduled staff conference
    B. discuss with the new employee the many problems which the kitchen staff faces daily
    C. give the new employee a task to see how well he can perform
    D. have a conference with the new employee and discuss what his duties will be

    23._____

24. Assume that, as part of a step-by-step training process, the supervisor explained and demonstrated a food preparation task to a new employee. As a last step, the supervisor told the employee to perform the task himself.
    The training given by this supervisor was

    24._____

A. *good;* by putting the employee on his own, the supervisor indicated confidence in the employee
B. *poor;* he didn't ask whether the employee understood how to perform the task
C. *good;* he employed the technique of demonstration
D. *poor;* more than one instructor is required to make this method of training effective

25. Of the following, the BEST way to follow-up immediately after giving a new employee training in food preparation tasks is to

    A. have the new employee observe more experienced employees performing their tasks
    B. give the new employee an overall view of all the food service operations
    C. allow the new employee to perform the tasks herself under careful supervision
    D. have the new employee write a report on what she has learned

26. If one of your kitchen staff performs a particularly important task incorrectly, the one of the following times which is BEST for teaching her the proper procedure so that she will remember it is

    A. later on in the day after she has had time to think about the task
    B. immediately so that she can correct her error
    C. after the workday ends so you may speak to her with less distraction
    D. during the next regularly-scheduled staff training session

27. Assume that you are approached by a cook who is upset and who wants to give you her explanation as to why the day's food preparation went wrong.
    In order to be an understanding listener, you should do ALL of the following EXCEPT

    A. carefully question the worker
    B. make a value judgment so you can take a definite position on the matter
    C. try to find out the meaning of the emotions behind the cook's statements
    D. restate the cook's position to assure that you comprehend what she is telling you

28. A troubled subordinate privately approaches his supervisor in order to talk about a problem on the job.
    In this situation, the one of the following actions that is NOT desirable on the part of the supervisor is to

    A. ask the subordinate pertinent questions to help develop points further
    B. close his office door during the talk to block noisy distractions
    C. allow sufficient time to complete the discussion with the subordinate
    D. take over the conversation so the employee won't be embarrassed

29. Suppose that one of your goals as a supervisor is to foster good working relationships between yourself and your employees, without undermining your supervisory effectiveness by being too friendly.
    Of the following, the BEST way to achieve this goal when dealing with employees' work problems is to

    A. discourage individual personal conferences by using regularly scheduled staff meetings to discuss work problems
    B. try to resolve work problems within a relatively short period of time

C. insist that employees put all work problems into writing before seeing you
D. maintain an open-door policy, allowing employees complete freedom of access to you without making appointments to discuss work problems

30. Of the following duties, the one that may be performed by a designated employee instead of the manager is   30._____

   A. preparing work schedules for each job in the kitchen
   B. placing all orders for food
   C. checking, counting, and weighing supplies received
   D. tasting all cooked foods, salads, sandwich and dessert mixtures

---

KEY (CORRECT ANSWERS)

1. A	11. A	21. C
2. C	12. C	22. D
3. D	13. B	23. D
4. C	14. C	24. B
5. A	15. D	25. C
6. C	16. D	26. B
7. B	17. B	27. B
8. D	18. A	28. D
9. D	19. C	29. B
10. C	20. D	30. C

EXAMINATION SECTION
TEST 1

DIRECTIONS: Each question or incomplete statement is followed by several suggested answers or completions. Select the one that BEST answers the question or completes the statement. *PRINT THE LETTER OF THE CORRECT ANSWER IN THE SPACE AT THE RIGHT.*

1. The one of the following entrees which offers the LEAST variation in texture is 1.____

   A. turkey, cranberry sauce, fried golden brown potatoes, peas
   B. chopped sirloin, mushroom gravy, French fried potatoes broccoli spears
   C. oven-fried chicken, baked potato, peas and carrots, salad
   D. meat loaf, mashed potatoes, creamed spinach, white bread

2. In planning a menu, the FIRST item which should be chosen is the 2.____

   A. vegetable B. salad C. entree D. dessert

3. Of the following, the BEST method of tenderizing cuts of meat which are less tender is by 3.____

   A. broiling B. stewing C. baking D. deep-frying

4. Which one of the following statements regarding proteins is CORRECT? 4.____

   A. The amount of protein in the body is a constant.
   B. The presence of nitrogen distinguishes protein from carbohydrates and fat.
   C. Protein provides more calories per gram than carbohydrates or fat.
   D. Protein provides the principal source of glucose to brain tissue.

5. The one of the following foods that provides MORE vitamin C per serving than the others is 5.____

   A. brussels sprouts B. cabbage
   C. tomatoes D. turnips

6. Liver is a PRIMARY source of which one of the following vitamins? 6.____

   A. A B. B_6 C. C D. D

7. Vitamin A is a fat soluble vitamin essential in an adequate diet for children and adults. Which one of the following statements concerning vitamin A is TRUE? 7.____

   A. The Recommended Daily Allowance for vitamin A for the adult male and female 10 years of age and older is the same.
   B. The Recommended Daily Allowance for vitamin A is expressed in terms of U.S.P. units.
   C. Vegetables have vitamin A activity equal to vitamin A in animal foods.
   D. Excessive amounts of vitamin A are well tolerated by adults.

8. Iron is a mineral required for growth and to keep the body functioning properly. Of the following, the combination of foods that will provide the BEST intake of iron is 8.____

   A. green peas, liver, enriched bread, dried potatoes
   B. cheese, oranges, liver, butter

C. peanut butter, milk, carrots, liver
D. liver, ice cream, chicken, peaches

9. Calcium and phosphorous account for approximately three-fourths of the mineral elements in the body. Their intake is important for adequate nutrition.
Which one of the following statements is CORRECT about both minerals?

   A. For children and young adults, the Recommended Daily Allowance for calcium is twice that for phosphorous.
   B. Their absorption and utilization are enhanced by the presence of vitamin E.
   C. They are not found in soft tissues.
   D. They constitute an important buffer system in the regulation of body neutrality.

10. When a menu is being planned for a specific holiday, the one of the following which is LEAST appropriate is to

    A. ask for suitable menu possibilities from the staff
    B. choose only foods which are familiar to those who will be served
    C. test acceptability of possible holiday items by serving one or two items at earlier meals
    D. include traditional foods associated with the holiday, if available

11. When a No. 8 scoop is used to serve mashed potatoes, the portion served should be _____ cup.

    A. 2/5   B. 1/3   C. 1/2   D. 2/3

12. A six-ounce ladle is equal to APPROXIMATELY _____ cup(s).

    A. 1/2   B. 1   C. 3/4   D. 1 1/4

13. The MOST accurate measurement of food is by

    A. volume
    B. weight
    C. can size
    D. number of pieces per container

14. Deep fat frying is BEST accomplished at which one of the following temperatures?

    A. 300° F   B. 350° F   C. 400° F   D. 450° F

15. When you are roasting beef, the indication that a well-done and palatable product has been achieved is an interior temperature in the range of

    A. 110° to 130° F   B. 131° to 150° F
    C. 151° to 170° F   D. 171° to 190° F

16. Of the following methods of roasting beef, the one that causes the LEAST amount of shrinkage is cooking at

    A. high temperature during the first half of the cooking time and at low temperature during the other half
    B. high temperature during the entire cooking time

C. moderate temperature during the first half of the cooking time and at high temperature during the other half
D. low temperature during the entire cooking time

17. The method of meat preparation that calls for cutting the meat into small pieces, covering with hot liquid, and cooking at about 185° F is known as   17.____

   A. boiling   B. stewing   C. roasting   D. broiling

18. Of the following pressure ranges, the one in which three compartment steamers operate is the _____ lb. range.   18.____

   A. 1-5   B. 5-15   C. 15-30   D. 30-50

19. When vegetables are cooked for large numbers of people, the BEST results are obtained by *batch cooking*.   19.____
    This kind of cooking is done in order to

   A. have high-quality vegetables available during the entire serving period
   B. prepare more vegetables using less staff
   C. use less equipment
   D. prepare several batches of vegetables at the same time

20. The one of the following procedures that could cause food poisoning is   20.____

   A. allowing cooked poultry to stand for an hour, slicing it, and covering it with broth, and holding it at room temperature for several hours
   B. keeping food mixtures on cafeteria counters for one hour
   C. cooking left-over food mixtures quickly by frequent stirring and then refrigerating in shallow pans
   D. chilling all ingredients for salads for at least one hour before preparation

21. When large numbers of people are to be served in a cafeteria setting, an estimate should be made each day of the quantity of food to be prepared and cooked.   21.____
    This is BEST done by which one of the following ways?

   A. Having the cook make a list of the previous day's leftovers.
   B. Considering previous sales of the same menu combinations, as well as the weather and any special events.
   C. Cooking as much food as the staff and equipment allow so as not to be caught short.
   D. Using the capacity of the seating area as a base.

22. Which one of the following statements concerning frozen pre-cooked foods is NOT correct?   22.____

   A. Certain pre-cooked foods are excellent when freshly prepared, but deteriorate rapidly in an ordinary freezer.
   B. Some pre-cooked foods are so greatly changed by freezing and subsequent reheating that they become unpalatable.
   C. All food items which are carefully cooked, rapidly frozen, and then held at low temperature until used, are satisfactory products when served.
   D. Many foods may be frozen, stored in an appropriate type of freezer, and thawed without marked change in nutritional and esthetic value.

23. Of the following, the one which is NOT a method of controlling food costs in an institutional food service is   23.____

   A. avoiding the use of *leftover* foods since they are usually unpopular items
   B. maintaining an accurate food inventory
   C. knowing what yield can be obtained from various sizes, counts, and amounts of food
   D. ensuring the food-service employees use standardized recipes and portions

24. The direct labor cost involved in the preparation of meals includes wages paid to cooks, bakers, salad makers, counter workers, etc. and is MOST accurately determined by which one of the following methods?   24.____

   A. Making studies of the amount of time spent by employees in actual meal preparation tasks.
   B. Checking employees' time cards to determine total absence time.
   C. Dividing the number of meals served each week by the number of employees.
   D. Determining how much time is lost because of equipment breakdown and adding the value of this time to the cost of employees' wages.

25. Which one of the following would MOST likely enable the supervisor of a food service to attain better cost control over operations?   25.____

   A. *Increasing* the output of individual staff members.
   B. *Increasing* the size of the staff.
   C. *Reducing* the amount of time scheduled for food preparation tasks.
   D. *Reducing* the amount of time spent on training staff members.

KEY (CORRECT ANSWERS)

1.	D	11.	C
2.	C	12.	C
3.	B	13.	B
4.	B	14.	B
5.	A	15.	D
6.	A	16.	D
7.	A	17.	B
8.	A	18.	B
9.	D	19.	A
10.	B	20.	A

21. B
22. C
23. A
24. A
25. A

TEST 2

DIRECTIONS: Each question or incomplete statement is followed by several suggested answers or completions. Select the one that BEST answers the question or completes the statement. *PRINT THE LETTER OF THE CORRECT ANSWER IN THE SPACE AT THE RIGHT.*

1. Of the following, the FIRST step in the control of food costs in an institution should be to   1.____

   A. make sure the delivery of foods is in accordance with the order
   B. store foods under tight security as soon as they are received
   C. follow purchase specifications in obtaining food products
   D. get the correct amount of raw food to the cook

2. Of the following, the area in which recipe costing aids are of MOST value is   2.____

   A. making yield studies
   B. planning menus
   C. taking inventories
   D. determining the cost of wasted foods

3. Control records of both the physical and cost aspects of food storage are MOST useful as a basic guide in which one of the following areas?   3.____

   A. Receiving food deliveries
   B. Issuing food to the kitchen
   C. Ordering food
   D. Controlling food theft

4. The one of the following which indicates actual control over food costs in a food service is that   4.____

   A. recipe costing is done
   B. waste is eliminated
   C. yield studies are made
   D. food cost data are regularly analyzed

5. The one of the following which is the MAJOR purpose of a perpetual inventory in the food storage area of a kitchen or other dietary unit is to   5.____

   A. facilitate removal of shelf items that are needed for quick use
   B. reduce breakage and spoilage of liquified foods
   C. act as a control in the area of food purchasing
   D. facilitate the planning of balanced diets and menus

6. Walk-in storage refrigerators can be a very important aspect of a well-equipped kitchen in a food service.
   Of the following, the MOST desirable location for a walk-in refrigerator is near the   6.____

   A. receiving and preparation areas
   B. tray delivery area
   C. cafeteria
   D. dishwashing area

7. Food specifications are precise statements of quality and other commodity requirements. All food should be purchased according to specifications.
Of the following, the LEAST important aspect of a food specification is the

   A. quantity required in a case, pound, carton, etc.
   B. federal grade desired
   C. size of the container
   D. picture of the item

8. The aim in buying food is to obtain the best value for the money spent.
Of the following, the practice which is LEAST likely to accomplish that aim is

   A. buying the cheapest item
   B. purchasing by specification
   C. purchasing only the quantities required for the menus planned
   D. checking all purchases on delivery

9. When deciding whether to select a particular piece of equipment for a kitchen or other dietary area, the one of the following which would be LEAST important for you to take into consideration is

   A. whether there is space for it
   B. whether it is easily cleaned and maintained
   C. whether there is an employee currently on staff who knows how to operate it
   D. how well it has worked in other institutions

10. Of the following foods, the type that is MOST likely to cause staph food poisoning if improperly prepared or handled is _____ food.

    A. sugar-coated   B. dried
    C. pickled   D. cream-filled

11. Harmful bacteria are MOST often introduced into foods prepared in a food service operation by

    A. insects   B. rodents   C. employees   D. utensils

12. When planning menus for secondary school students, it is desirable for the manager to do all of the following EXCEPT to

    A. stay within the school's food budget
    B. include familiar ethnic foods
    C. include many food choices
    D. consider the size of the food service staff

13. Of the following, the manager's BEST evidence for a shortage claim on surplus food delivered to a school is

    A. her written report of the shortage claim
    B. the delivery receipt from the truck driver
    C. the container the food was delivered in
    D. an old container of the same item

14. The manager should prepare school lunch menus for a MINIMUM of _____ week(s) at a time. 14._____

    A. one B. two C. three D. four

15. The manager must keep monthly inventories of all of the following EXCEPT 15._____

    A. paper goods B. food items
    C. serving utensils D. cleaning supplies

16. In the Type A lunch pattern for 10- to 12-year-old children, all of the following fulfill the *meat or meat alternate* requirement EXCEPT 16._____

    A. two ounces of cheese
    B. one-half cup of fresh carrots
    C. four tablespoons of peanut butter
    D. one-half cup of cooked dry peas

17. A manager is planning to use tuna fish salad to comply with the guideline for the *meat or meat alternate* requirement of the Type A lunch for secondary school students. How much tuna fish will she need in order to serve 400 secondary school students? _____ pounds. 17._____

    A. $37\frac{1}{2}$ B. 50 C. 75 D. 100

Questions 18-25.

DIRECTIONS: Answer Questions 18 through 25 SOLELY on the basis of information presented in the charts below.

STUDENT SALES COUNTER SHEET
March 4, 2005

Item	Price per Item	No. Items Offered for Sale	No. Items Unsold	Total Cash Received for Items Sold
Hot lunch	$2.25	250	75	
Milk	$0.60	525		$285.00
Soda	$0.75	300	163	$102.75
Ice Cream Bars	$0.45	181	59	$54.90
Buttered Roll	$0.15	200	150	
Cooked Vegetable	$0.90	325	40	$256.50
Pudding	$0.45	565	30	$240.75
Potato Chips	$0.30	610	50	$168.00

STUDENT SALES COUNTER SHEET
March 5, 2005

Item	Price per Item	No. Items Offered for Sale	No. Items Unsold	Total Cash Received for Items Sold
Hot lunch	$2.25	300		$585.00
Milk	$0.60	450		$255.00
Soda	$0.75	275	207	
Ice Cream Bars	$0.45	250	100	
Buttered Roll	$0.15	175	25	
Cooked Vegetable	$0.90	300	62	$214.20
Pudding	$0.45	490	47	
Potato Chips	$0.30	595	45	

18. Hot lunches accounted for APPROXIMATELY what percentage of all cash received for March 4, 2005?

    A. 10% B. 15% C. 20% D. 25%

19. Which one of the following items was sold LEAST on March 4, 2005 and March 5, 2005, combined?

    A. Soda
    B. Ice cream bars
    C. Buttered roll
    D. Cooked vegetable

20. The number of milk containers which were unsold on March 4, 2005 is

    A. 30 B. 50 C. 75 D. 95

21. How many fewer containers of pudding and soda were sold on March 5, 2005 than were sold on March 4, 2005?

    A. 19 B. 81 C. 105 D. 161

22. Which single item, besides hot lunches, accounted for the GREATEST number of items sold on March 4, 2005?

    A. Cooked vegetable
    B. Pudding
    C. Ice cream bars
    D. Soda

23. How many hot lunches were sold on March 4, 2005 and March 5, 2005, combined?

    A. 435 B. 550 C. 625 D. 665

24. Of the following, the item that was bought MOST by the students on both March 4, 2005 and March 5, 2005 is

    A. soda
    B. buttered roll
    C. pudding
    D. potato chips

25. The cumulative total of money received for all the soda, ice cream bars, buttered rolls, and pudding sold on March 4, 2005 is

    A. $165.15 B. $405.90 C. $858.90 D. $1252.65

KEY (CORRECT ANSWERS)

1. C
2. B
3. C
4. B
5. C

6. A
7. D
8. A
9. C
10. D

11. C
12. C
13. C
14. D
15. C

16. B
17. C
18. D
19. C
20. B

21. D
22. B
23. A
24. D
25. B

EXAMINATION SECTION
TEST 1

DIRECTIONS: Each question or incomplete statement is followed by several suggested answers or completions. Select the one that BEST answers the question or completes the statement. *PRINT THE LETTER OF THE CORRECT ANSWER IN THE SPACE AT THE RIGHT.*

1. Foods which are left over may be used by the menu planner CHIEFLY to 1.____

    A. baste meats
    B. stock the freezer with emergency supplies
    C. provide more variety in the next day's menu
    D. add minerals to the diet

2. When a recipe calls for cooking in a hot oven, it is MOST desirable to set the thermostat at a Fahrenheit temperature of 2.____

    A. 300°   B. 350°   C. 425°   D. 525°

3. Of the following, the MOST satisfactory method for cooking the less tender cuts of meat is by 3.____

    A. roasting   B. broiling   C. dry heat   D. moist heat

4. A two-pound chicken is BEST prepared by 4.____

    A. broiling   B. stewing   C. baking   D. roasting

5. Fats are used in food preparation, *not only* as emulsifiers, *but also* as 5.____

    A. shortening agents   B. leavening agents
    C. catalysts   D. sweetening agents

6. Baking powder is used in cake mixtures CHIEFLY in order to 6.____

    A. improve the flavor
    B. increase the acidity
    C. lighten the cake and increase its volume
    D. hold the other ingredients together

7. When making a sponge cake, it is important to remember to 7.____

    A. beat the batter until it doubles in bulk
    B. bake the cake in an ungreased tube pan
    C. bake the cake in a hot oven
    D. remove the cake from the pan as soon as it is baked

8. When making pastry, the fat should be 8.____

    A. creamed with the flour
    B. first melted and then creamed with the flour
    C. cut into the flour
    D. added to the flour after the water is stirred in

2 (#1)

9. Of the following, the procedure which is MOST advisable when cooking dried prunes is to

   A. soak the fruit in hot water to seal in the juices
   B. keep the uncooked fruit under refrigeration at all times
   C. simmer the fruit slowly until it is tender
   D. add sugar to the fruit to improve the flavor

9.____

10. Assume that you plan to serve a gelatin dessert for dinner. You have found that gelatin made in the usual way softens in hot weather.
    Of the following, the procedure which is MOST advisable to follow on a warm day is to

    A. thicken the gelatin with cornstarch
    B. substitute a non-gelatin dessert
    C. use fruit juice in the mixture
    D. use less water than usual

10.____

11. When preparing cream of tomato soup, it is MOST advisable to

    A. add hot milk slowly to cold tomato juice
    B. mix milk and tomato juice and then heat
    C. add cold tomato juice slowly to hot milk
    D. add cold milk slowly to hot tomato juice

11.____

12. In order to prevent cornstarch from lumping in cooking, it is MOST advisable to

    A. mix the starch with cold liquid before heating
    B. add hot liquid immediately to the starch
    C. brown the starch and add hot liquid
    D. heat the starch in a double boiler

12.____

13. Of the following, the LEAST desirable way to dry bread is to place it in

    A. uncovered pans on top of heated ovens
    B. paper bags which are suspended over the stoves
    C. deep pans in a warm oven
    D. cabinets which have slow heat

13.____

14. Of the following, the one which is a mollusk used in the preparation of soup is

    A. crab   B. oyster   C. lobster   D. cod

14.____

15. Whole dry milk is preferable to evaporated milk for use as a beverage CHIEFLY because it

    A. takes less time to prepare
    B. contains more vitamins
    C. can be made to look and taste more like whole milk
    D. contains more calories

15.____

16. The one of the following which is a RESIDUE-FREE food is

    A. milk   B. grapefruit sections
    C. lettuce   D. lemon gelatin

16.____

17. The one of the following which is NOT a legume is 17.____

   A. peanuts   B. okra   C. beans   D. lentils

18. Of the following, the sugar which is SWEETEST is 18.____

   A. lactose   B. fructose   C. sucrose   D. maltose

19. Broths are of value in the diet CHIEFLY because they are 19.____

   A. high in food value
   B. a good source of protein
   C. effective appetite stimulants
   D. a good source of carbohydrates

20. Of the following groups, the one which may be served on a SOFT diet is 20.____

   A. cream soup, mashed potato, spinach puree, toast, butter, custard
   B. broiled chicken, mashed potato, buttered peas, toast, milk
   C. vegetable soup, lamp chops, mashed potato, lettuce salad, toast
   D. clear broth, baked potato, tenderloin steak, carrots, apple pie

21. Of the following fruits, those which may be included in a HIGH ACID ash diet are 21.____

   A. prunes   B. oranges   C. bananas   D. pears

22. Of the following statements regarding yeast, the one which is MOST accurate is that 22.____
    yeast

   A. is generally harmful   B. changes starch to sugar
   C. lives without air   D. requires alcohol to live

23. The souring of milk is due PRIMARILY to the action of bacteria on 23.____

   A. fatty acids   B. proteins   C. amino acids   D. lactose

24. Glycerol, which is an end product of fat metabolism, is further oxidized in the body to 24.____

   A. sucrose   B. galactose   C. levulose   D. glucose

25. Cereals should be included in menus that are planned PRIMARILY to be 25.____

   A. weight reducing   B. low in starch
   C. low in cost   D. high in vitamin C

KEY (CORRECT ANSWERS)

1.	C	11.	C
2.	C	12.	A
3.	D	13.	A
4.	A	14.	B
5.	A	15.	C
6.	C	16.	D
7.	B	17.	B
8.	C	18.	B
9.	C	19.	C
10.	D	20.	A

21. A
22. B
23. D
24. D
25. C

TEST 2

DIRECTIONS: Each question or incomplete statement is followed by several suggested answers or completions. Select the one that BEST answers the question or completes the statement. *PRINT THE LETTER OF THE CORRECT ANSWER IN THE SPACE AT THE RIGHT.*

1. Of the following, a high blood sugar content is MOST likely to be a symptom of 1.____

    A. anemia
    B. diabetes mellitus
    C. arteriosclerosis
    D. hypertension

2. Trichinosis is a disease which may be caused by 2.____

    A. eating ham which has been overcooked
    B. unsanitary handling of frozen meats
    C. eating food which has been contaminated by infected flies
    D. eating infected pork which has been cooked insufficiently

3. Of the following, the bacteria which causes MOST food poisoning cases is 3.____

    A. botulinum   B. salmonella   C. pneumococci   D. streptococci

4. In the normal diet, liver should be used at least once a week since it is a GOOD source of 4.____

    A. vitamin C   B. phosphorus   C. iron   D. roughage

5. Water is important in the daily intake of the body CHIEFLY because it 5.____

    A. causes the oxidation of food in the body
    B. is a transporting medium for all body substances
    C. cools the air in the lungs
    D. gives off minerals when it is digested

6. Cod liver oil is given to children CHIEFLY in order to aid in 6.____

    A. absorption of calcium
    B. carbohydrate metabolism
    C. prevention of beriberi
    D. regulation of osmotic pressure

7. Of the following statements with respect to the nutritional needs of children, the one which is MOST accurate is that 7.____

    A. a child of four years of age requires a minimum of 2000 calories a day
    B. it is better for a child to be slightly underweight than to be overweight
    C. proportionately, children require more protein per pound of body weight than do adults
    D. a child whose diet is deficient in vitamin D may develop scurvy as a result

8. The one of the following desserts which it is MOST advisable to use in a low protein diet is 8.____

    A. rune soufflé
    B. fruit cup
    C. gelatin
    D. junket

53

9. The Karell diet is used in the care of

   A. Addison's disease
   B. cardiac conditions
   C. diabetes
   D. jaundice

10. Rowe elimination diets are used in cases involving

    A. allergy
    B. lead poisoning
    C. constipation
    D. nephritis

11. Of the following conditions, the one for which the normal diet is MODIFIED by restricting sodium is

    A. tuberculosis   B. diabetes   C. gastritis   D. edema

12. The one of the following conditions which may cause jaundice is

    A. faulty functioning of the kidneys
    B. an obstruction in the common bile duct
    C. a deficiency of vitamin C
    D. the presence of the yeast spore

13. It is GENERALLY accepted that exophthalmic goiter may result from

    A. the inability of the body to metabolize purines
    B. injury to the pancreas
    C. a diet deficient in iodine
    D. lack of sufficient sunlight and milk

14. Faulty ossification of the legs, ribs, and cranial bones are symptoms GENERALLY associated with

    A. pellagra   B. rickets   C. neuritis   D. encephalitis

15. Of the following diseases, the one which is characterized PRIMARILY by destruction of the liver cells is

    A. diabetes   B. leukemia   C. scurvy   D. cirrhosis

Questions 16-25.

DIRECTIONS: Column I lists 10 diseases or conditions, numbered 16 to 25, which require dietary treatment. Column II lists the dietary treatments which are generally used for the conditions listed in Column I. In the space at the right, opposite the number preceding each of the conditions in Column I, place the letter preceding the dietary treatment in Column II which is MOST appropriate for the condition in Column I.

COLUMN I

16. Addison's disease
17. cirrhosis
18. diabetes
19. exophthalmic goiter
20. gastric ulcer
21. gout
22. lipoid nephrosis
23. obesity
24. rickets
25. typhoid fever

COLUMN II

A. low carbohydrate diet
B. high caloric, non-stimulating diet
C. non-residue diet, high in protein and acid ash
D. diet high in vitamin C and magnesium
E. high protein, high carbohydrate, low roughage diet
F. high caloric, soft diet, given in small, frequent feedings
G. diet high in carbohydrate and vitamins, low in potassium, with added salt
H. diet with normal or high protein, vitamins, and minerals; low in fat and carbohydrate; low in caloric value
I. high protein and sulphur diet
J. low protein, purine-free diet
K. high protein, low fat diet, with limited sodium
L. diet high in protein and carbohydrate, low in fat, high in vitamin B complex
M. diet high in vitamin D

16. ____
17. ____
18. ____
19. ____
20. ____
21. ____
22. ____
23. ____
24. ____
25. ____

KEY (CORRECT ANSWERS)

1. B	11. D
2. D	12. B
3. B	13. C
4. C	14. B
5. B	15. D
6. A	16. G
7. C	17. L
8. B	18. A
9. B	19. B
10. A	20. F

21. J
22. K
23. H
24. M
25. E

EXAMINATION SECTION
TEST 1

DIRECTIONS: Each question or incomplete statement is followed by several suggested answers or completions. Select the one that BEST answers the question or completes the statement. *PRINT THE LETTER OF THE CORRECT ANSWER IN THE SPACE AT THE RIGHT.*

1. The one of the following which is the MOST important requirement of a good menu is that it

    A. include a large variety of food
    B. list foods which are well-liked
    C. be printed neatly on a clean menu card
    D. be suited to the purpose for which it is planned

2. Of the following, the procedure which is MOST desirable for proper tray service is to

    A. heat all dishes before placing them on the tray
    B. serve hot food hot, and cold food cold
    C. have all patients elevated in order to permit easier swallowing of food
    D. always serve iced water on the tray

3. The PROPER position for the knife on the tray is

    A. above the dinner plate
    B. across the bread and butter plate
    C. to the right of the dinner plate
    D. next to the fork

4. For attractive tray service, it is MOST advisable to serve harvard beets

    A. on the plate with the meat
    B. in a small side vegetable dish
    C. on a bed of shredded lettuce
    D. with a very thick, heavy sauce

5. The kitchen dietitian can work MOST efficiently if her office is located

    A. away from the kitchen, so she can be free from distractions
    B. in a central position where she may view all that happens
    C. at the entrance to the kitchen where she can see people entering and leaving
    D. next to the pantry, so she can see that no unauthorized person enters

6. The PRIMARY purpose of keeping records in the dietary department is to

    A. reduce waste in ordering food and supplies
    B. increase consumption of the most nutritious foods
    C. train subordinates in office techniques
    D. maintain statistical records of retail prices

7. A budget is BEST described as a(n)

   A. detailed plan for expenditures
   B. schedule for figuring depreciation of equipment over a period of years
   C. order for necessary equipment
   D. periodic accounting for past expenditures

8. Of the following, the CHIEF reason why a refrigerator door should NOT be left open is that the open door will

   A. stop the motor
   B. cause a drop in room temperature
   C. permit the cold air to rise to the top
   D. permit warm air to enter the refrigerator

9. Ovens with thermostatic heat controls should be

   A. kept closed at all times
   B. opened carefully to prevent jarring
   C. checked periodically for accuracy
   D. disconnected when not in use

10. The term *net weight* means MOST NEARLY the

    A. actual weight of an item
    B. weight of the container when empty
    C. combined weight of an item and its container
    D. estimated weight of the container alone

11. In requisitioning food, it is LEAST necessary for a dietitian to

    A. specify the exact quantity desired
    B. secure the signature of the cashier
    C. know the delivery times and order accordingly
    D. know the sizes in which foods are marketed

12. When receiving an order of food, it is INADVISABLE for the dietitian to

    A. check carefully against the order or requisition
    B. see that all fresh foods are weighed and checked in at the receiving room
    C. check for quality as well as quantity of foods delivered
    D. subtract two pounds tare from the weight of each package delivered in an order

13. Assume that, when inspecting a delivery of vegetables, you find a large amount of sorrel mixed in with a bushel of spinach.
    The one of the following actions which it is MOST advisable for you to take is to

    A. sort the spinach and sorrel in cleaning and cook them separately to allow greater variety in the menu
    B. discard the sorrel as waste
    C. call the purchasing office and arrange to return the spinach as unsatisfactory
    D. place the sorrel in the refrigerator and return it to the driver on his next delivery

14. When purchasing iceberg lettuce, it is ADVISABLE to look for lettuce which is

    A. loosely headed, with soft curly leaves and a yellow heart
    B. tightly headed, elongated, with coarse green leaves
    C. tightly headed, with medium green outside leaves and a pale green heart
    D. loosely headed, with elongated stalk and rugged curly leaves

15. The term *30-40 prunes* is used to describe the

    A. number of prunes in a box
    B. particular variety of prunes
    C. brand name of prunes
    D. number of prunes in a pound

16. When ordering chocolate liquor, the dietitian should expect to receive a _____ chocolate.

    A. solid piece of   B. semi-liquid
    C. liquid   D. glass jar of

17. Of the following, the BEST reason for discarding the green part of potatoes is that it contains a poison known as

    A. cevitamic acid   B. citric acid
    C. solanine   D. trichinae

18. The number of cans that a standard case of #10 canned apples USUALLY contains is

    A. 6   B. 12   C. 18   D. 24

19. Of the following, the person MOST closely associated with work in the field of infant behavior and feeding is

    A. H. Pollack   B. A. Gesell
    C. E.J. Stieglitz   D. J.F. Freeman

20. Of the following, the person BEST known for work in the field of diabetes is

    A. N. Jolliffe   B. H. Sherman
    C. R.M. Wilder   D. F. Stern

21. An egg which is strictly fresh will

    A. float in cold water
    B. have a thin and watery egg white
    C. have a swollen egg yolk which is easily broken
    D. sink in cold water

22. Cocoa and chocolate are rich in

    A. glycogen   B. gum   C. cellulose   D. starch

23. The percentage of protein that is usually converted into glucose in the body is MOST NEARLY

    A. 49%   B. 58%   C. 67%   D. 78%

24. Of the following vegetables, the one which gives the LARGEST yield, pound for pound, when pureed is

    A. fresh celery
    B. frozen peas
    C. frozen asparagus
    D. fresh carrots

25. If the composition of two small rib chops is Protein - 21 grams and Fat - 17 grams, the number of calories in the two chops is MOST NEARLY

    A. 136
    B. 200
    C. 237
    D. 257

KEY (CORRECT ANSWERS)

1. D
2. B
3. C
4. B
5. B

6. A
7. A
8. D
9. C
10. A

11. B
12. D
13. C
14. C
15. D

16. C
17. C
18. A
19. B
20. C

21. D
22. D
23. B
24. D
25. C

TEST 2

DIRECTIONS: Each question or incomplete statement is followed by several suggested answers or completions. Select the one that BEST answers the question or completes the statement. *PRINT THE LETTER OF THE CORRECT ANSWER IN THE SPACE AT THE RIGHT.*

1. An APPROPRIATE substitute for sucrose for a patient on a low carbohydrate diet is   1.____

    A. saccharin   B. casec   C. lactose   D. protinol

2. Of the following, the vegetables which are high in protein and, therefore, sometimes substituted for meat are   2.____

    A. green leafy vegetables   B. legumes
    C. root vegetables   D. gourds

3. When planning menus, it is *advisable* to use fish at least once a week because it is a GOOD source of   3.____

    A. iron   B. vitamin C   C. zinc   D. iodine

4. Of the following, the one which is a *non-nutritive* beverage is   4.____

    A. clear tea   B. orangeade
    C. oatmeal gruel   D. cream soda

5. Macaroni is *usually* used as a substitute for   5.____

    A. salad   B. meat   C. potato   D. dessert

6. Bread is dextrinized by   6.____

    A. toasting   B. chopping
    C. drying in open air   D. soaking in hot water

7. Baked custard is used on the menu CHIEFLY   7.____

    A. as a source of vitamin C
    B. because of its high protein content
    C. to add color
    D. as a source of starch

8. The one of the following which is a *non-irritating* food is   8.____

    A. cabbage   B. pickles   C. spaghetti   D. celery

9. Leaves of rhubarb and beets, when boiled in an aluminum container, will clean the container because they contain   9.____

    A. sulphuric acid   B. oxalic acid
    C. ammonia   D. alkali

10. When refinishing a refrigerator ice cube tray, the one of the following which should NOT be used as a coating material is   10.____

    A. aluminum   B. cadmium   C. tin   D. nickel

11. The Department of Health requires the sterilization of eating utensils by

    A. hot air sterilizers
    B. ultraviolet rays
    C. chemical solutions
    D. water at 180° F

12. Suppose that the dishwashing machine has become clogged with food particles. Of the following, the action which would be MOST advisable for the dietitian to take *first* is to

    A. call the service man to disassemble and clean the machine
    B. instruct the employees assigned to washing dishes about proper scraping of dishes
    C. order the employees to prerinse all dishes in order to prevent clogging
    D. remove the strainer tray

13. The one of the following which is the MOST effective way to rid a food storeroom of mice is to

    A. cement tight all holes which permit invasion
    B. set traps to catch the mice
    C. spread poison around the floor
    D. burn a sulphur candle in the storeroom

14. Black stoves are cleaned BEST by

    A. polishing with an oiled cloth
    B. rubbing with a piece of wax paper
    C. scrubbing with soap and water
    D. heating until they are red hot

15. Of the following, the BEST procedure for cleaning a red quarry tile floor in a hospital kitchen is to

    A. scrub it, then wax the floor
    B. hose it down with steam
    C. wash it with a strong soap
    D. wash it with a lye

16. After making ice cream, it is MOST important that the machine be

    A. rinsed thoroughly in cold water
    B. sterilized
    C. soaked in soap solution
    D. scrubbed with a brush

17. A dietitian assigned to work with clinic patients should have a basic knowledge of the foods of foreign-born people.
    Of the following, the MOST important reason for this is that

    A. it is interesting and exciting to eat the exotic dishes of foreign lands
    B. such knowledge would prove beyond doubt that poor diet is the cause of poor health among the foreign-born

C. such knowledge would help the dietitian to plan the patient's prescribed diet around familiar foods
D. many foreign dishes are more nutritious than American foods

18. The clinic dietitian meets several problems of the aging. The one of the following for which she is LEAST responsible is the

    A. detection of the onset of chronic degenerative diseases
    B. conservation of the health of the individual
    C. re-evaluation of the caloric requirements of aged patients
    D. overcoming of superstitions and food fallacies

18.____

19. When advising on methods of economizing, the clinic dietitian should instruct patients to AVOID buying

    A. foods in quantity, even though storage space permits
    B. foods that are in season and in abundance on the market
    C. less expensive cuts of meat
    D. butter, since there are less expensive substitutes on the market

19.____

20. The one of the following services which is the LEAST basic function of a nutrition clinic is to

    A. serve as a teaching center for students
    B. provide educational programs for patients of all ages
    C. follow up the nutritional status of individual patients
    D. secure diet histories of patients for the correction of undesirable food habits

20.____

21. Time and motion studies in the field of dietetics are used PRIMARILY to

    A. check on lateness and absence records of employees
    B. reduce effort and increase efficiency in performing particular tasks
    C. prepare estimates of time required between requisition and delivery dates
    D. schedule the daily work assignments for the entire staff

21.____

22. The PRIMARY purpose of using standardized recipes is to

    A. aid in controlling food costs
    B. encourage the cooks to try out new foods
    C. prepare large quantities of food
    D. determine the caloric values of foods

22.____

23. The CHIEF advantage of keeping a perpetual inventory of stock items is that

    A. supplies may be stored more easily
    B. there will be less breakage and loss of stock
    C. it makes it unnecessary to order replacements for stock supplies
    D. the balance on hand at any time is easily determined

23.____

24. In order to prevent the loss of vitamins in cooking, it is HOST advisable to

    A. cover the food completely with water while cooking and boil it rapidly
    B. peel and soak vegetables in cold water before cooking

24.____

C. dice vegetables into small pieces and boil them in an open pot
D. cook vegetables in the shortest possible time in a covered pot containing little water

25. To marinate is to   25.____

   A. let foods stand in a specially prepared liquid to add flavor or to tenderize them
   B. cook food in liquid just below the boiling point
   C. moisten food while cooking by pouring over it drippings or other liquids
   D. cook food in water at boiling temperature

KEY (CORRECT ANSWERS)

1. A	11. D
2. B	12. A
3. D	13. A
4. A	14. C
5. C	15. B
6. A	16. B
7. B	17. C
8. C	18. A
9. B	19. D
10. B	20. A

21. B
22. A
23. D
24. D
25. A

EXAMINATION SECTION
TEST 1

DIRECTIONS: Each question or incomplete statement is followed by several suggested answers or completions. Select the one that BEST answers the question or completes the statement. *PRINT THE LETTER OF THE CORRECT ANSWER IN THE SPACE AT THE RIGHT.*

1. Fuel value of foods is determined by use of a(n)
    A. caloric unit
    B. calorific unit
    C. calciferol
    D. calorimeter

2. Folacin is necessary for
    A. digestion of carbohydrates
    B. metabolism of sterols
    C. synthesis of chlorophyll
    D. hematopoiesis

3. Avidin is a(n)
    A. vitamin   B. protein   C. fiber   D. fabric

4. Baking powders are a mixture of cornstarch, baking soda, and a(n)
    A. acid   B. alkali   C. gas   D. neutralizer

5. The CORRECT method of cooking green-colored vegetables is to
    A. pressure cook
    B. add a small amount of baking soda
    C. release the steam occasionally while cooking in a covered saucepan
    D. keep the saucepan tightly covered

6. Popovers and cream puffs are PRINCIPALLY leavened by
    A. steam
    B. air
    C. carbon dioxide
    D. nitrous oxide

7. Compared with the recommended figure of 50%, the actual percentage of food calories derived from protective foods in the American diet is
    A. 20%   B. 25%   C. 33%   D. 45%

8. A bacteriostatic method of food preservation is
    A. open kettle canning
    B. pressure canning
    C. dehydration
    D. irradiation

9. For the average American, minerals of value as food supplements for the diet are calcium,
    A. phosphorus, sodium, and choline
    B. chlorine, magnesium, and iron
    C. phosphorus, iron, and iodine
    D. chlorine, iron, and manganese

10. For the average American, the vitamins of value as food supplements are thiamine, pyridoxine, riboflavin, calciferol, ascorbic acid, and

   A. niacin, B_{12}, A
   B. B_6, B_{12}, folic acid
   C. B_{12}, K and A
   D. B_{12}, A and E

11. The critical temperatures for eggs in storage are

   A. 28° and 68°
   B. 32° and 75°
   C. 38° and 60°
   D. 25° and 75°

12. When they are to form an ingredient in cake, eggs blend with the batter better if they are

   A. new laid
   B. chilled thoroughly
   C. brought to room temperature
   D. candled

13. Of the following, the HIGHEST in caloric value is 1 cupful

   A. strained honey
   B. orange juice
   C. sugar
   D. homogenized milk

14. Among the following, the BEST food source of thiamine is

   A. refined sugars
   B. fats
   C. egg white
   D. pork

15. In the list below, the BEST source of vitamin A is

   A. wheat germ   B. pork   C. milk   D. spinach

16. A disadvantage resulting from the intake of mineral oil is that it

   A. adds calories
   B. reduces weight
   C. impairs the appetite
   D. dissolves vitamin A

17. The leavening power of baking powders results from chemical action which releases

   A. carbon monoxide
   B. carbon dioxide
   C. cream of tartar
   D. lactic acid

18. The diet prescribed in diverticulitis is one that is

   A. high in calorie value
   B. high in roughage content
   C. low residue, bland
   D. high protein, bland

19. In typhoid fever, the diet should be

   A. *high* in calories and residue
   B. *low* in calories, high in residue
   C. *high* in calories, low in residue
   D. *high* in fruit juice content

20. Allspice is derived from   20._____

    A. the berry of the pimento tree
    B. a mixture of nutmeg, cinnamon and cloves
    C. the root of the allspice tree
    D. the bark of the cassia tree

21. Among the following food additives, the one which is used for the purpose of enhancing   21._____
    the keeping quality of the food is

    A. vitamin D in milk
    B. bleaching agents in flour
    C. ascorbic acid in cider
    D. minerals and vitamins in cereals

22. An example of the bactericidal method of food preservation is   22._____

    A. jam and jellies   B. pickling
    C. freezing   D. refrigeration

23. The material which destroys the activity of biotin is   23._____

    A. the protein found in uncooked egg white
    B. fluorides in drinking water
    C. iodides in medications
    D. fluorescent substances found in milk

24. Egg whites beat BEST if they are   24._____

    A. warm   B. chilled thoroughly
    C. at room temperature   D. beaten by hand

25. The RICHEST food sources of folacin are   25._____

    A. livers and green leafy vegetables
    B. eggs and milk
    C. cereals
    D. fats

KEY (CORRECT ANSWERS)

1. D
2. D
3. B
4. A
5. C

6. A
7. C
8. C
9. C
10. A

11. A
12. C
13. A
14. D
15. D

16. D
17. B
18. C
19. C
20. A

21. C
22. A
23. A
24. C
25. A

TEST 2

DIRECTIONS: Each question or incomplete statement is followed by several suggested answers or completions. Select the one that BEST answers the question or completes the statement. *PRINT THE LETTER OF THE CORRECT ANSWER IN THE SPACE AT THE RIGHT.*

1. Riboflavin is easily destroyed by   1.____
   - A. alkalies and light
   - B. acids and oxygen
   - C. heat and agitation
   - D. air and agitation

2. Cretinism is a form of idiocy due to extreme deficiency of secretion by   2.____
   - A. fat-soluble vitamins in the diet
   - B. B-complex vitamins in the diet
   - C. thyroid gland
   - D. adrenal glands

3. Nyctalopia results from a lack of   3.____
   - A. vitamin A
   - B. fluorine
   - C. citric acid
   - D. flavinoids

4. The MAJOR influence in the decline of endemic goiter in the United States is the use of   4.____
   - A. saffron oil
   - B. homogenized milk
   - C. iodized salt
   - D. enriched cereals

5. The Food Drug & Cosmetic Act of 1934 provides for   5.____
   - A. retention of nutritive values
   - B. fair pricing of goods
   - C. purity of content
   - D. accurate labeling

6. The liver is the storage depot in the body for vitamin   6.____
   - A. A
   - B. E
   - C. C
   - D. B

7. The anti-xerophthalmia vitamin is vitamin   7.____
   - A. A
   - B. B
   - C. E
   - D. K

8. The pathway of excretion of the nitrogenous end products of protein metabolism is the   8.____
   - A. lungs
   - B. skin
   - C. kidneys
   - D. large intestine

9. The term *trace elements* refers to   9.____
   - A. minerals needed in very small amounts in nutrition
   - B. substances which trace circulation in the body
   - C. tools used in sewing
   - D. potent drugs used as pain killer

10. Flavinoids which are effective in human health are

   A. biotics
   B. bioflavinoids
   C. neoflavinoids
   D. vitamins

11. Uric acid results from

   A. vitamin deficiency
   B. metabolism of purines
   C. digestion of carbohydrates
   D. injection of nicotine

12. Studies comparing the desirability of feeding to premature infants formulas warmed to body temperature and those given directly on removal from the refrigerator show

   A. no significant difference
   B. disturbed sleep following intake of cold formula
   C. regurgitation following intake of cold formula
   D. slower weight gain with cold feeding

13. Hypoglycemia is a condition of

   A. diseased eyes
   B. B, low blood sugar
   C. high blood sugar
   D. low purin content

14. The normal source of insulin in the human body is the

   A. liver
   B. thymus
   C. pancreas
   D. pineal gland

15. One of the earliest symptoms of a thiamine deficiency is

   A. polyneuritis
   B. anorexia
   C. nyctalopia
   D. conjunctivitis

16. Air is used as a leavening agent in

   A. sponge cake
   B. pound cake
   C. cookies
   D. bread

17. Cheese originates in

   A. pasteurization
   B. fermentation
   C. inversion
   D. coagulation

18. In measuring vitamin A value in foods, the International Unit is defined as the activity of

   A. 5.0 mg. calciferol
   B. 6.0 gm. tocopherol
   C. 6.0 gm. carotene
   D. 0.6 meg. betacarotene

19. In the last fifty years, the proportion of calories from milk, cheese, fruits, and vegetables in the American diet has

   A. remained the same
   B. doubled
   C. tripled
   D. quadrupled

20. Interference with absorption of vitamin A may result from   20._____

    A. a diet heavy with bulk foods
    B. overconsumption of salad oils
    C. mineral oil in salad dressings
    D. low cholesterol diet

21. Vitamin A food value is   21._____

    A. lacking in yams
    B. fairly constant in dairy products
    C. closely related to green coloring in vegetables
    D. closely related to sun available during growing time

22. The passage of digested substances into the villi for distribution through the body is called   22._____

    A. absorption   B. metabolism
    C. anabolism   D. peristalsis

23. Of the following, the RICHEST source of vitamin E is   23._____

    A. liver   B. green leafy vegetables
    C. wheat germ oil   D. egg yolk

24. Of the following, the number of calories which MOST NEARLY approximates the daily fuel needs of a moderately active 25-year-old woman is   24._____

    A. 1500   B. 2000   C. 2500   D. 3500

25. A deficiency of riboflavin results in   25._____

    A. xerophthalmia   B. polyneuritis
    C. cutaneous lesions   D. chielosis

KEY (CORRECT ANSWERS)

1.	A	11.	B
2.	C	12.	A
3.	A	13.	B
4.	C	14.	C
5.	D	15.	B
6.	A	16.	A
7.	A	17.	B
8.	C	18.	D
9.	A	19.	B
10.	B	20.	C

21. C
22. A
23. C
24. C
25. B

———

EXAMINATION SECTION
TEST 1

DIRECTIONS: Each question or incomplete statement is followed by several suggested answers or completions. Select the one that BEST answers the question or completes the statement. *PRINT THE LETTER OF THE CORRECT ANSWER IN THE SPACE AT THE RIGHT.*

1. The orientation of a new dietitian should include instruction in the primary goals of the hospital.
   The MOST important reason for this is that the dietitian

   A. should be able to explain the hospital goals to the kitchen and pantry workers if they ask her
   B. may be able to suggest improvements in hospital operations
   C. should be made to place the hospital's goals ahead of her own goals
   D. will be better motivated if she feels she is helping to fulfill the goals of the hospital

2. When training a new employee in a job procedure, it is LEAST desirable to

   A. give him an overall picture of the job and its importance
   B. stress key points when demonstrating the job
   C. have him do the first tryout of the job in your presence
   D. leave him alone once he has completed the tryout successfully

3. The method of training should be adapted to the situation. It is BEST to use the conference method, in which the trainees hold a guided discussion among themselves, for

   A. informing dietitians of a new procedure on requisitioning food
   B. instructing student nurses in the foods to be avoided on various therapeutic diets
   C. assisting dietitians to solve problems involving personnel grievances
   D. teaching stockroom workers the proper way of loading and unloading material

4. It is LEAST desirable to give detailed instruction sheets describing work procedures to

   A. cooks who are supervised directly and frequently
   B. kitchen helpers whose education is very limited
   C. storeroom workers who perform the tasks involved infrequently
   D. dietitians who are often called upon to exercise independent judgment

5. To be sure that an employee who is being trained actually understands his new job, it is BEST to

   A. repeat the training session with him on three successive days
   B. ask him if he understands all the instructions
   C. tell him to ask you if he does not understand any of the instructions
   D. have him repeat the instructions and perform the job

6. Several methods of judging the results of training are available to the head dietitian. The one of the following methods which is MOST useful as an indicator of whether a course in improving skills has been effective is to

A. ask the trainees their reaction to the course at the close of training
B. test the principles and techniques taught by giving an examination at the close of the training course
C. compare the subjects covered in the lesson plans for the course with the job analysis
D. compare the performance of trainees before and after training

7. A dietitian under your supervision has changed the assignment of a kitchen helper to a less desirable one because he was late twice in one week. You believe her action was premature, and the worker has complained to you of unfair treatment.
It would be BEST for you to

   A. support the dietitian's action when speaking to the helper, but later tell the dietitian to consult you before taking any disciplinary actions
   B. tell the helper that he is under the authority of the dietitian and must accept her decisions
   C. advise the helper that if his future attendance is good, you will see that his previous assignment is restored to him
   D. tell the helper to speak to the dietitian, and discuss privately with the dietitian the principles to follow in disciplining employees

7.____

8. Many grievances expressed against a supervisor actually originate outside the work situation; for example, a cook who is worried about his home life may work poorly and continually accuse the dietitian of treating him unfairly. In such a case, you should instruct the dietitian to

   A. keep out of the situation since her actions cannot eliminate the cause of the grievance
   B. advise the cook how to solve the situation which caused the grievance
   C. help the cook to understand that his home situation affects his attitude
   D. listen to the cook's grievance without comment, giving the cook a chance to relieve his tension harmlessly

8.____

9. A supervisor is not only part of management, she is also an intermediary with higher management for her subordinates. According to this principle, a head dietitian should

   A. refer employee grievances to higher management for settlement
   B. share with her subordinate employees information from higher management
   C. adapt department directives to meet the circumstances under which her subordinates work
   D. let higher management know of the feelings and desires of her subordinates

9.____

10. The mere fact that dietary employees do not complain about their work does not mean that there is a good relationship between them and the supervising dietitian. The BEST explanation of this is that

    A. a happy worker is usually more productive than a discontented one
    B. employees may nurse grievances silently if they do not trust the reaction of the dietitian to their expression
    C. although good relations between the dietitian and dietary employees are desirable, other motivations also spur productivity
    D. we have not yet succeeded in understanding fully why employees act the way they do

10.____

11. Assume that the kitchen workers often complain of great fatigue at the end of the day. Your FIRST step should be to

    A. arrange the work schedule to allow rest periods toward the end of the day
    B. arrange the work schedule to have the more fatiguing tasks performed early in the day
    C. obtain more specific facts about where and when fatigue occurs
    D. determine if complaints come from workers who have complained of other working conditions

12. Although you have previously indicated that a dietitian under your supervision should make decisions on her own, she continues asking for your opinion when it is not necessary.
    It would be BEST for you to

    A. continue answering her questions until she feels, capable of making decisions herself
    B. inform her that your function is to supervise her, not to make decisions for her
    C. be less demanding so that she will not fear to make decisions
    D. lead her gradually into making decisions more frequently

13. Employee acceptance of a comprehensive new procedure is MOST likely if the head dietitian

    A. consults the employees when beginning work on the procedure
    B. consults the employees when the procedure is fully formulated
    C. incorporates in the procedure a feature which will benefit the employees
    D. convinces the employees that the procedure will not be made final until it is tried out

14. Because there is a shortage of workers, two cooperative employees assigned to take monthly physical inventory in the food storeroom must also do other tasks and, therefore, continually complete the inventories late. The constant failure to complete the task on time has changed their original enthusiasm for their jobs to discontent.
    It would be BEST for you to

    A. assign no other work to them until each month's inventory is completed
    B. rotate the assignment so that no employee has it too often
    C. make the employees realize you do not blame them for their failure
    D. set the goal for the completion of the inventories at dates the employees can meet

15. An activities report of the dietary department is submitted each month. Several employees are assigned to complete the different parts of the report, a clerk computes the figures, and a typist prepares the final copy. The report is frequently submitted late, although little actual time is involved in the preparation.
    The reason for the delays is BEST ascertained by use of a(n) _____ chart.

    A. line organization   B. line and staff organization
    C. flow process   D. employee function

16. In planning a menu for patients, it is LEAST advisable to

   A. include a crisp, a firm, and a soft food for variety in texture
   B. serve foods which are plain and well-cooked in preference to fancy foods or mixed food combinations
   C. combine flavorful foods with milder ones, in preference to several highly seasoned foods
   D. have foods of one color, for less confusion and greater interest and attractiveness

17. Assume that a dietitian has submitted the following four dinner menus for inclusion in a master menu.
The one which BEST demonstrates the basic rules of good menu planning is:

   A. Tomato juice, fried chicken, French fried potatoes, buttered green beans, vegetable relish, bread and butter, jelly doughnuts, coffee, tea or milk
   B. Fruit juice cocktail, baked pork chops with cinnamon applesauce, whipped potatoes, Waldorf salad on lettuce, bread and butter, deep dish apple pie, coffee, tea or mil
   C. Cream of vegetable soup, baked haddock fillet, steamed potatoes, buttered cauliflower, celery hearts, bread and butter, vanilla ice cream, coffee, tea or milk
   D. Vegetable juice, roast beef with natural gravy, mashed potatoes, buttered spinach, corn relish, bread and butter, chilled canned peaches, coffee, tea or milk

18. A head dietitian in a main kitchen must be constantly alert in order to insure that food is being prepared properly for service.
For this purpose, it is LEAST important that she

   A. check periodically the time employees begin cooking foods
   B. determine if hot foods are being kept hot and cold foods kept cold
   C. see that the perpetual inventory is posted daily
   D. see that scales are being used for weighing ingredients when needed

19. When setting up standard recipes, it is LEAST desirable _____ for

   A. the amount of ingredients to be listed in weights and measures
   B. the ingredients to be listed in order of use
   C. each recipe to be set up for 100 portions
   D. fresh food items to be listed as A.P. or E.P.

20. When submitting requisitions for food items, the variety, size, quality, pack, and quantity desired should be specified.
Of the following items for requisitions, the one which LACKS necessary information is:

   A. Apples: fresh, McIntosh, 150 per box (approx. 2 1/2" in diam.), Grade A, 80 pounds
   B. Squash: fresh, Grade A, 3 to 5 pound average, in baskets or boxes, 150 pounds
   C. Potatoes: white, Idaho-baking, Grade A, 4 to 6 oz. each, 40 lbs. per box, 6 boxes
   D. Carrots: fresh, Western, topped, Grade B, 2" max. 3/4" min. dia., in sacks, 200 pounds

KEY (CORRECT ANSWERS)

1.	D	11.	C
2.	D	12.	D
3.	C	13.	A
4.	B	14.	D
5.	D	15.	C
6.	D	16.	D
7.	D	17.	D
8.	C	18.	C
9.	D	19.	C
10.	B	20.	B

TEST 2

DIRECTIONS: Each question or incomplete statement is followed by several suggested answers or completions. Select the one that BEST answers the question or completes the statement. *PRINT THE LETTER OF THE CORRECT ANSWER IN THE SPACE AT THE RIGHT.*

1. Disregarding the cost of labor, it is MORE economical to buy the unprocessed food when   1.___

    A. medium eggs for baking are 76 cents per dozen and frozen whole eggs are 76 cents per pound
    B. fresh peas in the pod are 15 cents per pound and frozen peas are 44 cents per pound
    C. 100 pounds of potatoes in skins are $12 and 30 pounds of peeled potatoes are $3.80
    D. fresh juice oranges are 24 cents per pound and frozen (concentrated) orange juice is $1.50 per 32-ounce can

2. When buying canned foods, it is BEST to purchase an item which is used frequently in large quantities if the   2.___

    A. purchase price per unit would be reduced as a result
    B. space for storage would not be affected to any extent
    C. item is popular with patients and employees
    D. unit-price reduction would be greater than the increase in storage and distribution costs

3. The foods listed below have been ordered for a dinner menu for 350 patients.   3.___
   The one which has been ordered in the MOST NEARLY CORRECT quantity is:

    A. boneless roast beef, 115 lbs.
    B. precooked rice for buttered rice, 15 lbs.
    C. white pearl onions for creamed onions, 200 lbs.
    D. fresh asparagus for buttered asparagus, 50 lbs,

4. Assume that you are serving 4 ounces of pineapple juice for breakfast.   4.___
   The number of cases of 46 ounce cans you would require for 260 employees and 560 patients is

    A. 4   B. 6   C. 10   D. 12

5. Assume that you are to serve 225 employees, 290 patients, 55 staff members.   5.___
   If a #10 can yields 32 servings of applesauce, the number of cases to requisition is

    A. 1   B. 3   C. 4   D. 10

6. You are ordering eviscerated frying chickens to serve a meal of fried chicken to approximately 900 patients and 850 employees.   6.___
   The MOST approximate amount to order is _____ .

    A. 600   B. 1500   C. 2000   D. 2500

7. Of the following vegetables, the one which is MOST acceptable on delivery is 7.____

   A. heads of lettuce with 4 or 5 crisp green wrapper leaves on them
   B. broccoli heads with tips of bright yellow showing through
   C. topped carrots that have new sprouts showing on the top
   D. salad greens, such as escarole and chicory, that have a small seed stem in the middle of the head

8. The fresh vegetable which has the GREATEST percentage of waste in preparation is 8.____

   A. cabbage   B. celery   C. cauliflower   D. lettuce

9. The tenderness of fryers may BEST be judged by the 9.____

   A. firmness of the flesh   B. flexibility of the breastbone
   C. absence of pinfeathers   D. weight of the fryers

10. Of the following temperatures for storing fresh foods, the LEAST desirable is 10.____

    A. 32° F. for lettuce   B. 34° F. for beef
    C. 40° F. for eggs   D. 65° F. for bananas

11. Assume that dishes are to be washed and rinsed in a dishwashing machine and then air-dried. 11.____
    The temperature of the water should be _____ F. for wash and _____ F. for rinse.

    A. 160° ; 200°   B. 180° ; 120°   C. 140° ; 150°   D. 140° ; 180°

12. If you are asked to help plan a storeroom for staples and canned goods, you should specify all of the following EXCEPT 12.____

    A. a concrete floor with suitable drainage
    B. a room free from machinery, ventilating ducts, and water pipes
    C. enough natural light to allow supplies to be seen easily
    D. only one door, opening into the kitchen

13. If Swiss steak is to be served, it is BEST to use 13.____

    A. beef rib   B. beef loin
    C. bottom round   D. top sirloin

14. The head dietitian must be concerned with efficiency and with the quality of foods. 14.____
    In establishing standard food preparation procedures, it is BEST to recommend that

    A. salad greens for lunch be prepared the previous evening and chilled
    B. potatoes for baking not be sorted by size, to save time and to provide for individual patient preferences
    C. cooked vegetables be placed in the steam table half an hour before the start of the meal to improve the flavor
    D. coffee be made fresh for each meal

15. In order to use a standardized recipe for apple pie throughout the year, it would be BEST to use 15.____

    A. frozen apples
    B. fresh sliced apples

C. fresh apples of the same variety
D. canned apples of the same brand name and code number

16. When preparing food, it is LEAST desirable to

    A. bake pie shells at 400° F
    B. cook egg custard (in water bath) at 325° F
    C. roast prime ribs of beef at 425° F
    D. bake layer cake at 350° F

17. When cooking a tough roast of beef, the method of cooking which should NOT be used is to

    A. add a little water to the meat and simmer in a covered pan
    B. cook uncovered on a rack in a roaster in the oven
    C. sear until brown and then cook in a pressure cooker
    D. brown, add tomato juice, and simmer in a covered pan

18. When the fat in a deep fat fryer is not hot enough, doughnuts in the fryer

    A. become soaked with fat
    B. lose their shape
    C. become too soft
    D. develop a dark brown color

19. In order to make BEST use of a deep fat fryer when cooking potatoes, the cook should be instructed to

    A. fill the fry basket to capacity and place it in the fryer as soon as the fryer is lighted
    B. fill the fry basket to capacity and place it in the fryer when the fat has been heated to the proper temperature
    C. put potatoes in several layers on the bottom of the fry basket and place the basket in the fryer as soon as the fryer is lighted
    D. put potatoes in several layers on the bottom of the fry basket and place the basket in the fryer when the fat has been heated to the proper cooking temperature

20. When using a coffee urn, it is IMPROPER to

    A. empty the water jacket around the coffee urn after cleaning the urn so that it can dry out thoroughly
    B. draw off coffee into the urn cup and repour through the filter again after water has dripped through the coffee filter
    C. see that the water is boiling before it flows over the coffee grounds into the urn
    D. keep the coffee from boiling after it has been made

KEY (CORRECT ANSWERS)

1. A
2. D
3. A
4. B
5. B

6. B
7. A
8. C
9. B
10. A

11. D
12. C
13. C
14. D
15. D

16. C
17. B
18. A
19. D
20. A

EXAMINATION SECTION
TEST 1

DIRECTIONS: Each question or incomplete statement is followed by several suggested answers or completions. Select the one that BEST answers the question or completes the statement. *PRINT THE LETTER OF THE CORRECT ANSWER IN THE SPACE AT THE RIGHT.*

1. Which of the following is the MOST likely action a supervisor should take to help establish an effective working relationship with his departmental superiors?
   A. Delay the implementation of new procedures received from superiors in order to evaluate their appropriateness.
   B. Skip the chain of command whenever he feels that it is to his advantage
   C. Keep supervisors informed of problems in his area and the steps taken to correct them
   D. Don't take up superiors' time by discussing anticipated problems but wait until the difficulties occur

   1.____

2. Of the following, the action a supervisor could take which would generally be MOST conducive to the establishment of an effective working relationship with employees includes
   A. maintaining impersonal relationships to prevent development of biased actions
   B. treating all employees equally without adjusting for individual differences
   C. continuous observation of employees on the job with insistence on constant improvement
   D. careful planning and scheduling of work for your employees

   2.____

3. Which of the following procedures is the LEAST likely to establish effective working relationships between employees and supervisors?
   A. Encouraging two-way communication with employees
   B. Periodic discussion with employees regarding their job performance
   C. Ignoring employees' gripes concerning job difficulties
   D. Avoiding personal prejudices in dealing with employees

   3.____

4. Criticism can be used as a tool to point out the weak areas of a subordinate's work performance.
   Of the following, the BEST action for a supervisor to take so that his criticism will be accepted is to
   A. focus his criticism on the act instead of on the person
   B. exaggerate the errors in order to motivate the employee to do better
   C. pass judgment quickly and privately without investigating the circumstances of the error
   D. generalize the criticism and not specifically point out the errors in performance

   4.____

5. In trying to improve the motivation of his subordinates, a supervisor can achieve the BEST results by taking action based upon the assumption that most employees
   A. have an inherent dislike of work
   B. wish to be closely directed
   C. are more interested in security than in assuming responsibility
   D. will exercise self-direction without coercion

6. When there are conflicts or tensions between top management and lower-level employees in any department, the supervisor should FIRST attempt to
   A. represent and enforce the management point of view
   B. act as the representative of the workers to get their ideas across to management
   C. serve as a two-way spokesman, trying to interpret each side to the other
   D. remain neutral, but keep informed of changes in the situation

7. A probationary period for new employees is usually provided in many agencies. The MAJOR purpose of such a period is usually to
   A. allow a determination of employee's suitability for the position
   B. obtain evidence as to employee's ability to perform in a higher position
   C. conform to requirements that ethnic hiring goals be met for all positions
   D. train the new employee in the duties of the position

8. An effective program of orientation for new employees usually includes all of the following EXCEPT
   A. having the supervisor introduce the new employee to his job, outlining his responsibilities and how to carry them out
   B. permitting the new worker to tour the facility or department so he can observe all parts of it in action
   C. scheduling meetings for new employees, at which the job requirements are explained to them and they are given personnel manuals
   D. testing the new worker on his skills and sending him to a centralized in-service workshop

9. In-service training is an important responsibility of many supervisors. The MAJOR reason for such training is to
   A. avoid future grievance procedures because employees might say they were not prepared to carry out their jobs
   B. maximize the effectiveness of the department by helping each employee perform at his full potential
   C. satisfy inspection teams from central headquarters of the department
   D. help prevent disagreements with members of the community

10. There are many forms of useful in-service training. Of the following, the training method which is NOT an appropriate technique for leadership development is to
    A. provide special workshops or clinics in activity skills
    B. conduct institutes to familiarize new workers with the program of the department and with their roles

C. schedule team meetings for problem-solving, including both supervisors and leaders
D. have the leader rate himself on an evaluation form periodically

11. Of the following techniques of evaluating work training programs, the one that is BEST is to
    A. pass out a carefully designed questionnaire to the trainees at the completion of the program
    B. test the knowledge that trainees have both at the beginning of training and at its completion
    C. interview the trainees at the completion of the program
    D. evaluate performance before and after training for both a control group and an experimental group

12. Assume that a new supervisor is having difficulty making his instructions to subordinates clearly understood.
    The one of the following which is the FIRST step he should take in dealing with this problem is to
    A. set up a training workshop in communication skills
    B. determine the extent and nature of the communications gap
    C. repeat both verbal and written instructions several times
    D. simplify his written and spoken vocabulary

13. A director has not properly carried out the orders of his assistant supervisor on several occasions to the point where he has been successively warned, reprimanded, and severely reprimanded.
    When the director once again does not carry out orders, the PROPER action for the assistant supervisor to take is to
    A. bring the director up on charges of failing to perform his duties properly
    B. have a serious discussion with the director, explaining the need for the orders and the necessity for carrying them out
    C. recommend that the director be transferred to another district
    D. severely reprimand the director again, making clear that no further deviation will be countenanced

14. A supervisor with several subordinates becomes aware that two of these subordinates are neither friendly nor congenial.
    In making assignments, it would be BEST for the supervisor to
    A. disregard the situation
    B. disregard the situation in making a choice of assignment but emphasize the need for teamwork
    C. investigate the situation to find out who is at fault and give that individual the less desirable assignments until such time as he corrects his attitude
    D. place the unfriendly subordinates in positions where they have as little contact with one another as possible

15. A DESIRABLE characteristic of a good supervisor is that he should
    A. identify himself with his subordinates rather than with higher management
    B. inform subordinates of forthcoming changes in policies and programs only when they directly affect the subordinates' activities
    C. make advancement of the subordinates contingent on personal loyalty to the supervisor
    D. make promises to subordinates only when sure of the ability to keep them

16. The supervisor who is MOST likely to be successful is the one who
    A. refrains from exercising the special privileges of his position
    B. maintains a formal attitude toward his subordinates
    C. maintains an informal attitude toward his subordinates
    D. represents the desires of his subordinate to his superiors

17. Application of sound principles of human relations by a supervisor may be expected to _____ the need for formal discipline.
    A. decrease
    B. have no effect on
    C. increase
    D. obviate

18. The MOST important generally approved way to maintain or develop high morale in one's subordinates is to
    A. give warnings and reprimands in a jocular way
    B. excuse from staff conferences those employees who are busy
    C. keep them informed of new developments and policies of higher management
    D. refrain from criticizing their faults directly

19. In training subordinates, an IMPORTANT principle for the supervisor to recognize is that
    A. a particular method of instruction will be of substantially equal value for all employees in a given title
    B. it is difficult to train people over 50 years of age because they have little capacity for learning
    C. persons undergoing the same course of training will learn at different rates of speed
    D. training can seldom achieve its purpose unless individual instruction is the chief method used

20. Over an extended period of time, a subordinate is MOST likely to become and remain most productive if the supervisor
    A. accords praise to the subordinate whenever his work is satisfactory, withholding criticism except in the case of very inferior work
    B. avoids both praise and criticism except for outstandingly good or bad work performed by the subordinate
    C. informs the subordinate of his shortcomings, as viewed by management, while according praise only when highly deserved
    D. keeps the subordinate informed of the degree of satisfaction with which his performance of the job is viewed by management.

KEY (CORRECT ANSWERS)

1.	C	11.	D
2.	D	12.	B
3.	C	13.	A
4.	A	14.	D
5.	D	15.	D
6.	C	16.	D
7.	A	17.	A
8.	D	18.	C
9.	B	19.	C
10.	D	20.	D

TEST 2

DIRECTIONS: Each question or incomplete statement is followed by several suggested answers or completions. Select the one that BEST answers the question or completes the statement. *PRINT THE LETTER OF THE CORRECT ANSWER IN THE SPACE AT THE RIGHT.*

1. A supervisor has just been told by a subordinate, Mr. Jones, that another employee, Mr. Smith, deliberately disobeyed an important rule of the department by taking home some confidential departmental material.
Of the following courses of action, it would be MOST advisable for the supervisor FIRST to
   A. discuss the matter privately with both Mr. Jones and Mrs. Smith at the same time
   B. call a meeting of the entire staff and discuss the matter generally without mentioning any employee by name
   C. arrange to supervise Mr. Smith's activities more closely
   D. discuss the matter privately with Mr. Smith

1.____

2. The one of the following actions which would be MOST efficient and economical for a supervisor to take to minimize the effect of periodical fluctuations in the workload of his unit is to
   A. increase his permanent staff until it is large enough to handle the work of the busy loads
   B. request the purchase of time- and labor-saving equipment to be used primarily during the busy loads
   C. lower, temporarily, the standards for quality of work performance during peak loads
   D. schedule for the slow periods work that is not essential to perform during the busy periods

2.____

3. Discipline of employees is usually a supervisor's responsibility. There may be several useful forms of disciplinary action.
Of the following, the form that is LEAST appropriate is the
   A. written reprimand or warning
   B. involuntary transfer to another work setting
   C. demotion or suspension
   D. assignment of added hours of work each week

3.____

4. Of the following, the MOST effective means of dealing with employee disciplinary problems is to
   A. give personality tests to individuals to identify their psychological problems
   B. distribute and discuss a policy manual containing exact rules governing employee behavior
   C. establish a single, clear penalty to be imposed for all wrongdoing irrespective of degree
   D. have supervisors get to know employees well through social mingling

4.____

5. A recently developed technique for appraising work performance is to have the supervisor record on a continual basis all significant incidents in each subordinate's behavior that indicate unsuccessful action and those that indicate poor behavior.
Of the following, a MAJOR disadvantage of this method of performance appraisal is that it
   A. often leads to overly close supervision
   B. results in competition among those subordinates being evaluated
   C. tends to result in superficial judgments
   D. lacks objectivity for evaluating performance

6. Assume that you are a supervisor and have observed the performance of an employee during a period of time. You have concluded that his performance needs improvement.
In order to improve his performance, it would, therefore, be BEST for you to
   A. note your findings in the employee's personnel folder so that his behavior is a matter of record
   B. report the findings to the personnel officer so he can take prompt action
   C. schedule a problem-solving conference with the employee
   D. recommend his transfer to simpler duties

7. When an employee's absences or latenesses seem to be nearing excessiveness, the supervisor should speak with him to find out what the problem is.
Of the following, if such a discussion produces no reasonable explanation, the discussion usually BEST serves to
   A. affirm clearly the supervisor's adherence to proper policy
   B. alert other employees that such behavior is unacceptable
   C. demonstrate that the supervisor truly represents higher management
   D. notify the employee that his behavior is being observed and evaluated

8. Assume that an employee willfully and recklessly violates an important agency regulation. The nature of the violation is of such magnitude that it demands immediate action, but the facts of the case are not entirely clear. Further, assume that the supervisor is free to make any of the following recommendations.
The MOST appropriate action for the supervisor to take is to recommend that the employee be
   A. discharged   B. suspended
   C. forced to resign   D. transferred

9. Although employees' titles may be identical, each position in that title may be considerably different.
Of the following, a supervisor should carefully assign each employee to a specific position based PRIMARILY on the employee's
   A. capability   B. experience   C. education   D. seniority

10. The one of the following situations where it is MOST appropriate to transfer an employee to a similar assignment is one in which the employee
    A. lacks motivation and interest
    B. experiences a personality conflict with his supervisor
    C. is negligent in the performance of his duties
    D. lacks capacity or ability to perform assigned tasks

10.____

11. The one of the following which is LEAST likely to be affected by improvements in the morale of personnel is employee
    A. skill
    B. absenteeism
    C. turnover
    D. job satisfaction

11.____

12. The one of the following situations in which it is LEAST appropriate for a supervisor to delegate authority to subordinates is where the supervisor
    A. lacks confidence in his own abilities to perform certain work
    B. is overburdened and cannot handle all his responsibilities
    C. refers all disciplinary problems to his subordinate
    D. has to deal with an emergency or crisis

12.____

13. Assume that it has come to your attention that two of your subordinates have shouted at each other and have almost engaged in a fist fight. Luckily, they were separated by some of the other employees.
    Of the following, your BEST immediate course of action would generally be to
    A. reprimand the senior of the two subordinates since he should have known better
    B. hear the story from both employees and any witnesses and then take needed disciplinary action
    C. ignore the matter since nobody was physically hurt
    D. immediately suspend and fine both employees pending a departmental hearing

13.____

14. You have been delegating some of your authority to one of your subordinates because of his leadership potential.
    Which of the following actions is LEAST conducive to the growth and development of this individual for a supervisory position?
    A. Use praise only when it will be effective
    B. Give very detailed instructions and supervise the employee closely to be sure that the instructions ae followed precisely
    C. Let the subordinate proceed with his planned course of action even if mistakes, within a permissible range, are made
    D. Intervene on behalf of the subordinate whenever an assignment becomes difficult for him

14.____

15. A rumor has been spreading in your department concerning the possibility of layoffs due to decreased revenues.
    As a supervisor, you should GENERALLY
    A. deny the rumor, whether it is true or false, in order to keep morale from declining

15.____

4 (#2)

    B. inform the men to the best of your knowledge about this situation and keep them advised of any new information
    C. tell the men to forget about the rumor and concentrate on increasing their productivity
    D. ignore the rumor since it is not authorized information

16. Within an organization, every supervisor should know to whom he reports and who reports to him.
    The one of the following which is achieved by use of such structured relationships is
    A. unity of command
    B. confidentiality
    C. esprit de corps
    D. promotion opportunities

16.____

17. Almost every afternoon, one of your employees comes back from his break ten minutes late without giving you any explanation.
    Which of the following actions should you take FIRST in this situation?
    A. Assign the employee to a different type of work and observe whether his behavior changes
    B. Give the employee extra work to do so that he will have to return on time
    C. Ask the employee for an explanation for his lateness
    D. Tell the employee he is jeopardizing the break for everyone

17.____

18. When giving instructions to your employees in a group, which one of the following should you make certain to do?
    A. Speak in a casual, off-hand manner
    B. Assume that your employees fully understand the instructions
    C. Write out your instructions beforehand and read them to the employees
    D. Tell exactly who is to do what

18.____

19. A fist fight develops between two men under your supervision.
    The MOST advisable course of action for you to take FIRST is to
    A. call the police
    B. have the other workers pull them apart
    C. order them to stop
    D. step between the two men

19.____

20. You have assigned some difficult and unusual work to one of your most experienced and competent subordinates.
    If you notice that he is doing the work incorrectly, you should
    A. assign the work to another employee
    B. reprimand him in private
    C. show him immediately how the work should be done
    D. wait until the job is completed and then correct his errors

20.____

KEY (CORRECT ANSWERS)

1.	D	11.	A
2.	D	12.	C
3.	D	13.	B
4.	B	14.	B
5.	A	15.	B
6.	C	16.	A
7.	D	17.	C
8.	B	18.	D
9.	A	19.	C
10.	B	20.	C

EXAMINATION SECTION
TEST 1

DIRECTIONS: Each question or incomplete statement is followed by several suggested answers or completions. Select the one that BEST answers the question or completes the statement. *PRINT THE LETTER OF THE CORRECT ANSWER IN THE SPACE AT THE RIGHT.*

1. Following are three statements concerning on-the-job training:
   I. On-the-job training is rarely used as a method of training employees.
   II. On-the-job training is often carried on with little or no planning.
   III. On-the-job training is often less expensive than other types.
   Which of the following BEST classifies the above statements into those that are correct and those that are not?
   A. I is correct, but II and III are not.
   B. II is correct but I and III are not.
   C. I and II are correct, but III is not.
   D. II and III are correct, but I is not.

   1.____

2. The one of the following which is NOT a valid principle for a supervisor to keep in mind when talking to a subordinate about his performance is:
   A. People frequently know when they deserve criticism.
   B. Supervisors should be prepared to offer suggestions to subordinates about how to improve their work.
   C. Good points should be discussed before bad points.
   D. Magnifying a subordinate's faults will get him to improve faster.

   2.____

3. In many organizations information travels quickly through the grapevine. Following are three statements concerning the *grapevine*:
   I. Information a subordinate does not want to tell her supervisor may reach the supervisor through the *grapevine*.
   II. A supervisor can often do her job better by knowing the information that travels through the *grapevine*.
   III. A supervisor can depend on the *grapevine* as a way to get accurate information from the employees on his staff.
   Which one of the following CORRECTLY classifies the above statements into those which are generally correct and those which are not?
   A. II is correct, but I and III are not.
   B. III is correct, but I and II are not.
   C. I and II are correct, but III is not.
   D. I and III are correct, but II is not.

   3.____

4. Following are three statements concerning supervision:
   I. A supervisor knows he is doing a good job if his subordinates depend upon him to make every decision.
   II. A supervisor who delegates authority to his subordinates soon finds that his subordinates begin to resent him.
   III. Giving credit for good work is frequently an effective method of getting subordinates to work harder

   4.____

Which one of the following CORRECTLY classifies the above statements into those that are correct and those that are not?
A. I and II are correct, but III is not.
B. II and III are correct, but I is not.
C. II is correct, but I and III are not.
D. III is correct, but I and II are not.

5. Of the following, the LEAST appropriate action for a supervisor to take in preparing a disciplinary case against a subordinate is to
   A. keep careful records of each incident in which the subordinate has been guilty of misconduct or incompetency, even though immediate disciplinary action may not be necessary
   B. discuss with the employee each incident of misconduct as it occurs so the employee knows where he stands
   C. accept memoranda from any other employees who may have been witnesses to acts of misconduct
   D. keep the subordinate's personnel file confidential so that he is unaware of the evidence being gathered against him

6. Praise by a supervisor can be an important element in motivating subordinates. Following are three statements concerning a supervisor's praise of subordinates:
   I. In order to be effective, praise must be lavish and constantly restated.
   II. Praise should be given in a manner which meets the needs of the individual subordinate.
   III. The subordinate whose work is praised should believe that the praise is earned.
   Which of the following CORRECTLY classifies the above statements into those that are correct and those that are not?
   A. I is correct, but II and III are not.
   B. II and III are correct, but I is not.
   C. III is correct, but I and II are not.
   D. I and II are correct, but III is not.

7. A supervisor feels that he is about to lose his temper while reprimanding a subordinate.
   Of the following, the BEST action for the supervisor to take is to
   A. postpone the reprimand for a short time until his self-control is assured
   B. continue the reprimand because a loss of temper by the supervisor will show the subordinate the seriousness of the error he made
   C. continue the reprimand because failure to do so will show that the supervisor does not have complete self-control
   D. postpone the reprimand until the subordinate is capable of understanding the reason for the supervisor's loss of temper

8. Following are three statements concerning various ways of giving orders to subordinates:
   I. An implied order or suggestion is usually appropriate for the inexperienced employee.
   II. A polite request is less likely to upset a sensitive subordinate than a direct order.
   III. A direct order is usually appropriate in an emergency situation.

Which of the following CORRECTLY classifies the above statements into those that are correct and those that are not?
- A. I is correct, but II and III are not.
- B. II and III are correct, but I is not.
- C. III is correct, but I and II are not.
- D. I and II are correct, but III is not.

9. The one of the following which is NOT an acceptable reason for taking disciplinary action against a subordinate guilty of serious violations of the rules is that
    - A. the supervisor can *let off steam* against subordinates who break rules frequently
    - B. a subordinate whose work continues to be unsatisfactory may be terminated
    - C. a subordinate may be encouraged to improve his work
    - D. an example is set for other employees

10. At the first meeting with your staff after appointment as a supervisor, you find considerable indifference and some hostility among the participants.
    Of the following, the MOST appropriate way to handle this situation is to
    - A. disregard the attitudes displayed and continue to make your presentation until you have completed it
    - B. discontinue your presentation but continue the meeting and attempt to find out the reasons for their attitudes
    - C. warm up your audience with some good-natured statements and anecdotes and then proceed with your presentation
    - D. discontinue the meeting and set up personal interviews with the staff members to try to find out the reason for their attitude

11. Use a written rather than oral communication to amend any previous written communication.
    Of the following, the BEST justification for this statement is that
    - A. oral changes will be considered more impersonal and thus less important
    - B. oral changes will be forgotten or recalled indifferently
    - C. written communications are clearer and shorter
    - D. written communications are better able to convey feeling tone

12. Assume that a certain supervisor, when writing important communications to his subordinates, often repeats certain points in different words.
    This technique is GENERALLY
    - A. *ineffective*; it tends to confuse rather than help
    - B. *effective*; it tends to improve understanding by the subordinates
    - C. *ineffective*; it unnecessarily increases the length of the communication and may annoy the subordinates
    - D. *effective*; repetition is always an advantage in communications

13. In preparing a letter or a report, a supervisor may wish to persuade the reader of the correctness of some idea or course of action.
    The BEST way to accomplish this is for the supervisor to
    - A. encourage the reader to make a prompt decision
    - B. express each idea in a separate paragraph

C. present the subject matter of the letter in the first paragraph
D. state the potential benefits for the reader

14. Effective communications, a basic necessity for successful supervision is a two-way street. A good supervisor needs to listen to, as well as disseminate, information and he must be able to encourage his subordinates to communicate with him.
Which of the following suggestions will contribute LEAST to improving the *listening power* of a supervisor?
    A. Don't assume anything; don't anticipate, and don't let a subordinate think you know what he is going to say
    B. Don't interrupt; let him have his full say even if it requires a second session that day to get the full story
    C. React quickly to his statements so that he knows you are interested, even if you must draw some conclusions prematurely
    D. Try to understand the real need for his talking to you even if it is quite different from the subject under discussion

15. Of the following, the MOST useful approach for the supervisor to take toward the informal employee communications network known as the *grapevine* is to
    A. remain isolated from it, but not take any active steps to eliminate it
    B. listen to it, but not depend on it for accurate information
    C. use it to disseminate confidential information
    D. eliminate it as diplomatically as possible

16. If a supervisor is asked to estimate the number of employees that he believes he will need in his unit in the coming fiscal year, the supervisor should FIRST attempt to learn the
    A. nature and size of the workload his unit will have during that time
    B. cost of hiring and training new employees
    C. average number of employee absences per year
    D. number of employees needed to indirectly support or assist his unit

17. An important supervisory responsibility is coordinating the operations of the unit. This may include setting work schedules, controlling work quality, establishing interim due dates, etc. In order to handle this task, it has been divided into the following five stages:
    I. <u>Determine the steps</u> or sequence required for the tasks to be performed.
    II. <u>Give the orders</u>, either written or oral, to begin work on the tasks.
    III. <u>Check up</u> by following each task to make sure it is proceeding according to plan.
    IV. <u>Schedule the jobs</u> by setting a time for each task of operation to begin and end.
    V. <u>Control the process</u> by correcting conditions which interfere with the plan.
    The MOST logical sequence in which these planning steps should be performed is:
    A. I, II, III, IV, V   B. II, I, V, III, IV   C. I, IV, II, III, V   D. IV, I, II, III, V

18. Assume that a supervisor calls a meeting with the staff under his supervision in order to discuss several proposals. After some discussion, he realizes that he strongly disagrees with one proposal that four of the staff have rather firmly favored.
At this point, he could BEST handle the situation by saying:
    A. *I have the responsibility for this decision, and I must disagree.*
    B. *I am just reminding you that I have had a great deal more experience in these matters.*
    C. *You have presented some good points, but perhaps we could look at it another way.*
    D. *The only way that this proposal can be disposed of is to defer it for further discussion.*

19. As far as the social activities and groups of his subordinates are concerned, a supervisor in a large organization can BEST strengthen his tools of leadership by
    A. emphasizing the organization as a whole and forbidding the formation of groups
    B. ignoring the groups as much as possible and dealing with each subordinate as an individual
    C. learning about the status structure of employee groups and their values
    D. avoiding any relationship with groups

20. If a subordinate asks you, his superior, for advice in planning his career in the department, you should
    A. encourage him to feel that he can easily reach the top of his occupational ladder
    B. discourage him from setting his hopes too high
    C. discuss career opportunities realistically with him
    D. explain that you have no control over his opportunities for advancement

21. A supervisor's evaluation of an employee is usually based upon a combination of objective facts and subjective judgments or opinions.
Which of the following aspects of an employee's work or performance is MOST likely to be subjectively evaluated?
    A. Quantity   B. Accuracy   C. Attitude   D. Attendance

22. Of the following possible characteristics of supervisors, the one MOST likely to lead to failure as a supervisor is
    A. a tendency to seek several opinions before making decisions in complex matters
    B. lack of a strong desire to advance to a top position in management
    C. little formal training in human relations skills
    D. poor relations with subordinates and other supervisory personnel

23. People who break rules do so for a number of reasons. However, employees will break rules LESS often if
    A. the supervisor uses his own judgment about work methods
    B. the supervisor pretends to act strictly, but isn't really serious about it
    C. they greatly enjoy their work
    D. they have completed many years of service

24. Assume that an employee under your supervision has become resentful and generally non-cooperative after his request for transfer to another office closer to his place of residence was denied. The request was denied primarily because of the importance of his current assignment. The employee has been a valued worker, but you are now worried that his resentful attitude will have a detrimental effect.
    Of the following, the MOST desirable way for you to handle this situation is to
    A. arrange for the employee's transfer to the office he originally requested
    B. arrange for the employee's transfer to another office, but not the one he originally requested
    C. attempt to re-focus the employee's attention on those aspects of his current assignment which will be most rewarding and satisfying to him
    D. explain to the employee that, while you are sympathetic to his request, department rules will not allow transfers for reasons of personal convenience

25. Of the following, it would be LEAST advisable for a supervisor to use his administrative authority to affect the behavior and activities of his subordinates when he is trying to
    A. change the way his subordinates perform a particular task
    B. establish a minimum level of conformity to established rules
    C. bring about change in the attitudes of his subordinates
    D. improve the speed with which his subordinates respond to his orders

26. Assume that a supervisor gives his subordinate instructions which are appropriate and clear. The subordinate thereupon refuses to follow these instructions.
    Of the following, it would then be MOST appropriate for the supervisor to
    A. attempt to find out what it is that the employee objects to
    B. take disciplinary action that same day
    C. remind the subordinate about supervisory authority and threaten him with discipline
    D. insist that the subordinate carry out the order immediately

27. Of the following, the MOST effective way to identify training needs resulting from gradual changes in procedure is to
    A. monitor on a continuous basis the actual jobs performed and the skills required
    B. periodically send out a written questionnaire asking personnel to identify their needs
    C. conduct interviews at regular intervals with selected employees
    D. consult employees' personnel records

28. Assume that you, as a supervisor, have had a new employee assigned to you. 28.____
If the duties of his position can be broken into independent parts, which of the following is usually the BEST way to train this new employee?
Start with
    A. the easiest duties and progressively proceed to the most difficult
    B. something easy; move to something difficult; then back to something easy
    C. something difficult; move to something easy; then to something difficult
    D. the most difficult duties and progressively proceed to the easiest

29. The oldest and most commonly used training technique is on-the-job training. 29.____
Instruction is given to the worker by his supervisor or by another employee. Such training is essential in most jobs, although it is not always effective when used alone.
This technique, however, can be effectively used alone if
    A. the skills involved can be learned quickly
    B. a large number of people are to be trained at one time
    C. other forms of training have not been previously used with the people involved
    D. the skills to be taught are mental rather than manual

30. It is generally agreed that the learning process is facilitated in proportion to 30.____
the amount of feedback that the learner is given about his performance.
Following are three statements concerning the learning process:
  I. The more specific the learner's knowledge of how he performed, the more rapid his improvement and the higher his level of performance
  II. Giving the learner knowledge of his results does not affect his motivation to learn.
  III. Learners who are not given feedback will set up subjective criteria and evaluate their own performance.
Which of the following choices lists ALL of the above statements that are generally CORRECT?
    A. I and II only   B. I and III only   C. II and III only   D. I, II, and III

KEY (CORRECT ANSWERS)

1.	D	11.	B	21.	C
2.	D	12.	B	22.	D
3.	C	13.	D	23.	C
4.	D	14.	C	24.	C
5.	D	15.	B	25.	C
6.	B	16.	A	26.	A
7.	A	17.	C	27.	A
8.	B	18.	C	28.	A
9.	A	19.	C	29.	A
10.	D	20.	C	30.	B

TEST 2

DIRECTIONS: Each question or incomplete statement is followed by several suggested answers or completions. Select the one that BEST answers the question or completes the statement. *PRINT THE LETTER OF THE CORRECT ANSWER IN THE SPACE AT THE RIGHT.*

Questions 1-6.

DIRECTIONS: Questions 1 through 6 are to be answered SOLELY on the basis of the information given in the following paragraph.

    The use of role-playing as a training technique was developed during the past decade by social scientists, particularly psychologists, who have been active in training experiments. Originally, this technique was applied by clinical psychologists who discovered that a patient appears to gain understanding of an emotionally disturbing situation when encouraged to act out roles in that situation. As applied in government and business organizations, the purpose of role-playing is to aid employees to understand certain work problems involving interpersonal relations and to enable observers to evaluate various reactions to them. Thus, for example, on the problem of handling grievances, two individuals from the group might be selected to act out extemporaneously the parts of subordinate and supervisor. When this situation is enacted by various pairs among the class and the techniques and results are discussed, the members of the group are presumed to reach conclusions about the most effective means of handling similar situations. Often the use of role reversal, where participants take parts different from their actual work roles, assists individuals to gain more insight into other people's problems and viewpoints. Although role-playing can be a rewarding training device, the trainer must be aware of his responsibilities. If this technique is to be successful, thorough briefing of both actors and observers as to the situation in question, the participants' roles, and what to look for, is essential.

1. The role-playing technique was FIRST used for the purpose of
   A. measuring the effectiveness of training programs
   B. training supervisors in business organizations
   C. treating emotionally disturbed patients
   D. handling employee grievances

1.____

2. When role-playing is used in private business as a training device, the CHIEF aim is to
   A. develop better relations between supervisor and subordinate in the handling of grievances
   B. come up with a solution to a specific problem that has arisen
   C. determine the training needs of the group
   D. increase employee understanding of the human relation factors in work situations

2.____

3. From the above passage, it is MOST reasonable to conclude that when role-playing is used, it is preferable to have the roles acted out by
   A. only one set of actors   B. no more than 2 sets of actors
   C. several different sets of actors   D. the trainer or trainers of the group

3.____

4. Based on the above passage, a trainer using the technique of role reversal in a problem of first-line supervision should assign a senior employee to play the part of a(n)
   A. new employee
   B. senior employee
   C. principal employee
   D. angry citizen

4.____

5. It can be inferred from the above passage that a limitation of role-play as a training method is that
   A. many work situations do not lend themselves to role-play
   B. employees are not experienced enough as actors to play the roles realistically
   C. only trainers who have psychological training can use it successfully
   D. participants who are observing and not acting do not benefit from it

5.____

6. To obtain good results from the use of role-playing in training, a trainer should give participants
   A. a minimum of information about the situation so that they can act spontaneously
   B. scripts which illustrate the best method for handling the situation
   C. a complete explanation of the problem and the roles to be acted out
   D. a summary of work problems which involve interpersonal relations

6.____

7. Of the following, the MOST important reason for a supervisor to prepare good written reports is that
   A. a supervisor is rated on the quality of his reports
   B. decisions are often made on the basis of the reports
   C. such reports take less time for superiors to review
   D. such reports demonstrate efficiency of department operations

7.____

8. Of the following, the BEST test of a good report is whether it
   A. provides the information needed
   B. shows the good sense of the writer
   C. is prepared according to a proper format
   D. is grammatical and neat

8.____

9. When a supervisor writes a report, he can BEST show that he has an understanding of the subject of the report by
   A. including necessary facts and omitting non-essential details
   B. using statistical data
   C. giving his conclusions but not the data on which they are based
   D. using a technical vocabulary

9.____

10. Suppose you and another supervisor on the same level are assigned to work together on a report. You disagree strongly with one of the recommendations the other supervisor wants to include in the report but you cannot change his views.
    Of the following, it would be BEST that
    A. you refuse to accept responsibility for the report
    B. you ask that someone else be assigned to this project to replace you

10.____

C. each of you state his own ideas about this recommendation in the report
D. you give in to the other supervisor's opinion for the sake of harmony

11. Standardized forms are often provided for submitting reports. 11.____
Of the following, the MOST important advantage of using standardized forms for reports is that
    A. they take less time to prepare than individually written reports
    B. necessary information is less likely to be omitted
    C. the responsibility for preparing these reports can be delegated to subordinates
    D. the person making the report can omit information he considers unimportant

12. A report which may BEST be classed as a *periodic* report is one which 12.____
    A. requires the same type of information at regular intervals
    B. contains detailed information which is to be retained in permanent records
    C. is prepared whenever a special situation occurs
    D. lists information in graphic form

13. Which one of the following is NOT an important reason for keeping accurate records in an office? 13.____
    A. Facts will be on hand when decisions have to be made.
    B. The basis for past actions can be determined.
    C. Information needed by other bureaus can be furnished.
    D. Filing is easier when records are properly made out.

14. Suppose you are preparing to write a report recommending a change in a certain procedure. You learn that another supervisor made a report a few years ago suggesting a change in this same procedure, but that no action was taken. 14.____
Of the following, it would be MOST desirable for you to
    A. avoid reading the other supervisor's report so that you will write with a more up-to-date point of view
    B. make no recommendation since management seems to be against any change in the procedure
    C. read the other report before you write your report to see what bearing it may have on your recommendations
    D. avoid including in your report any information that can be obtained by referring to the other report

15. If a report you are preparing to your superior is going to be a very long one, it would be DESIRABLE to include a summary of your basic conclusions 15.____
    A. at the end of the report
    B. at the beginning of the report
    C. in a separate memorandum
    D. right after you present the supporting data

16. Suppose that some bureau and department policies must be very frequently applied by your subordinates while others rarely come into use.
As a supervising employee, a GOOD technique for you to use in fulfilling your responsibility of seeing to it that policies are adhered to is to
    A. ask the director of the bureau to issue to all employees an explanation in writing of all policies
    B. review with your subordinates every week those policies which have daily application
    C. follow up on and explain at regular intervals the application of those policies which are not used very often by your subordinates
    D. recommend to your superiors that policies rarely used be changed or dropped

16.____

17. The BASIC purpose behind the principle of delegation of authority is to
    A. give the supervisor who is delegating a chance to acquire skills in higher level functions
    B. free the supervisor from routine tasks in order that he may do the important parts of his job
    C. prevent supervisors from overstepping the lines of authority which have been established
    D. place the work delegated in the hands of those employees who can perform it best

17.____

18. A district commander can BEST assist management in long-range planning by
    A. reporting to his superiors any changing conditions in the district
    B. maintaining a neat and efficiently run office
    C. scheduling work so that areas with a high rate of non-compliance get more intensive coverage
    D. properly training new personnel assigned to his district

18.____

19. Suppose that new quarters have been rented for your district office.
Of the following, the LEAST important factor to be considered in planning the layout of the office is the
    A. need for screening confidential activities from unauthorized persons
    B. relative importance of the various types of work
    C. areas of noise concentration
    D. convenience with which communication between sections of the office can be achieved

19.____

20. Of the following, the MOST basic effect of organizing a department so that lines of authority are clearly defined and duties are specifically assigned is to
    A. increase the need for close supervision
    B. decreases the initiative of subordinates
    C. lessen the possibility of duplication of work
    D. increase the responsibilities of supervisory personnel

20.____

21. An accepted management principle is that decisions should be delegated to the lowest point in the organization at which they can be made effectively.
The one of the following which is MOST likely to be a result of the application of this principle is that
   A. no factors will be overlooked in making decisions
   B. prompt action will follow the making of decisions
   C. decisions will be made more rapidly
   D. coordination of decisions that are made will be simplified

22. Suppose you are a supervisor and need some guidance from a higher authority. In which one of the following situations would it be PERMISSIBLE for you to bypass the regular upward channels of communication in the chain of command?
   A. In an emergency when your superior is not available
   B. When it is not essential to get a quick reply
   C. When you feel your immediate superior is not understanding of the situation
   D. When you want to obtain information that you think your superior does not have

23. Of the following, the CHIEF limitation of the organization chart as it is generally used in business and government is that the chart
   A. makes lines of responsibility and authority undesirably definite and formal
   B. is often out of date as soon as it is completed
   C. does not show human factors and informal working relationships
   D. is usually too complicated

24. The *span of control* for any supervisor is the
   A. number of tasks he is expected to perform himself
   B. amount of office space he and his subordinates occupy
   C. amount of work he is responsible for getting out
   D. number of subordinates he can supervise effectively

25. Of the following duties performed by a supervising employee, which would be considered a LINE function rather than a staff function?
   A. Evaluation of office personnel
   B. Recommendations for disciplinary action
   C. Initiating budget requests for replacement of equipment
   D. Inspections, at irregular times, of conditions and staff in the field

KEY (CORRECT ANSWERS)

1.	C	11.	B
2.	D	12.	A
3.	C	13.	D
4.	A	14.	C
5.	A	15.	B
6.	C	16.	C
7.	B	17.	B
8.	A	18.	A
9.	A	19.	B
10.	C	20.	C

21.	B
22.	A
23.	C
24.	D
25.	D

RECORD KEEPING
EXAMINATION SECTION
TEST 1

DIRECTIONS: Each question or incomplete statement is followed by several suggested answers or completions. Select the one that BEST answers the question or completes the statement. *PRINT THE LETTER OF THE CORRECT ANSWER IN THE SPACE AT THE RIGHT.*

Questions 1-7.

DIRECTIONS: In answering Questions 1 through 7, use the following master list. For each question, determine where the name would fit on the master list. Each answer choice indicates right before or after the name in the answer choice.

    Aaron, Jane
    Armstead, Brendan
    Bailey, Charles
    Dent, Ricardo
    Grant, Mark
    Mars, Justin
    Methieu, Justine
    Parker, Cathy
    Sampson, Suzy
    Thomas, Heather

1. Schmidt, William
   A. Right before Cathy Parker
   B. Right after Heather Thomas
   C. Right after Suzy Sampson
   D. Right before Ricardo Dent

1.____

2. Asanti, Kendall
   A. Right before Jane Aaron
   B. Right after Charles Bailey
   C. Right before Justine Methieu
   D. Right after Brendan Armstead

2.____

3. O'Brien, Daniel
   A. Right after Justine Methieu
   B. Right before Jane Aaron
   C. Right after Mark Grant
   D. Right before Suzy Sampson

3.____

4. Marrow, Alison
   A. Right before Cathy Parker
   B. Right before Justin Mars
   C. Right before Mark Grant
   D. Right after Heather Thomas

4.____

5. Grantt, Marissa
   A. Right before Mark Grant
   B. Right after Mark Grant
   C. Right after Justin Mars
   D. Right before Suzy Sampson

5.____

6. Thompson, Heath   6._____
   A. Right after Justin Mars   B. Right before Suzy Sampson
   C. Right after Heather Thomas   D. Right before Cathy Parker

DIRECTIONS: Before answering Question 7, add in all of the names from Questions 1 through 6. Then fit the name in alphabetical order based on the new list.

7. Francisco, Mildred   7._____
   A. Right before Mark Grant   B. Right after Marissa Grantt
   C. Right before Alison Marrow   D. Right after Kendall Asanti

Questions 8-10.

DIRECTIONS: In answering Questions 8 through 10, compare each pair of names and addresses. Indicate whether they are the same or different in any way.

8. William H. Pratt, J.D.   William H. Pratt, J.D.   8._____
   Attourney at Law   Attorney at Law
   A. No differences   B. 1 difference
   C. 2 differences   D. 3 differences

9. 1303 Theater Drive,; Apt. 3-B   1330 Theatre Drive,; Apt. 3-B   9._____
   A. No differences   B. 1 difference
   C. 2 differences   D. 3 differences

10. Petersdorff, Briana and Mary   Petersdorff, Briana and Mary   10._____
    A. No differences   B. 1 difference
    C. 2 differences   D. 3 differences

11. Which of the following words, if any, are misspelled?   11._____
    A. Affordable   B. Circumstansial
    C. Legalese   D. None of the above

Questions 12-13.

DIRECTIONS: Questions 12 and 13 are to be answered on the basis of the following table.

Standardized Test Results for High School Students in District #1230

	English	Math	Science	Reading
High School 1	21	22	15	18
High School 2	12	16	13	15
High School 3	16	18	21	17
High School 4	19	14	15	16

The scores for each high school in the district were averaged out and listed for each subject tested. Scores of 0-10 are significantly below College Readiness Standards. 11-15 are below College Readiness, 16-20 meet College Readiness, and 21-25 are above College Readiness.

12. If the high schools need to meet or exceed in at least half the categories in order to NOT be considered "at risk," which schools are considered "at risk"? 12._____
    A. High School 2
    B. High School 3
    C. High School 4
    D. Both A and C

13. What percentage of subjects did the district as a whole meet or exceed College Readiness standards? 13._____
    A. 25%   B. 50%   C. 75%   D. 100%

Questions 14-15.

DIRECTIONS: Questions 14 and 15 are to be answered on the basis of the following information.

You have seven employees working as a part of your team: Austin, Emily, Jeremy, Christina, Martin, Harriet, and Steve. You have just sent an e-mail informing them that there will be a mandatory training session next week. To ensure that work still gets done, you are offering the training twice during the week: once on Tuesday and also on Thursday. This way half the employees will still be working while the other half attend the training. The only other issue is that Jeremy doesn't work on Tuesdays and Harriet doesn't work on Thursdays due to compressed work schedules.

14. Which of the following is a possible attendance roster for the first training session? 14._____
    A. Emily, Jeremy, Steve
    B. Steve, Christina, Harriet
    C. Harriet, Jeremy, Austin
    D. Steve, Martin, Jeremy

15. If Harriet, Christina, and Steve attend the training session on Tuesday, which of the following is a possible roster for Thursday's training session? 15._____
    A. Jeremy, Emily, and Austin
    B. Emily, Martin, and Harriet
    C. Austin, Christina, and Emily
    D. Jeremy, Emily, and Steve

Questions 16-20.

DIRECTIONS: In answering Questions 16 through 20, you will be given a word and will need to choose the answer choice that is MOST similar or different to the word.

16. Which word means the SAME as *annual*? 16._____
    A. Monthly   B. Usually   C. Yearly   D. Constantly

17. Which word means the SAME as *effort*? 17._____
    A. Energy   B. Equate   C. Cherish   D. Commence

18. Which word means the OPPOSITE of *forlorn*? 18._____
    A. Neglected   B. Lethargy   C. Optimistic   D. Astonished

19. Which word means the SAME as *risk*? 19._____
    A. Admire   B. Hazard   C. Limit   D. Hesitant

20. Which word means the OPPOSITE of *translucent*?
    A. Opaque   B. Transparent   C. Luminous   D. Introverted

21. Last year, Jamie's annual salary was $50,000. Her boss called her today to inform her that she would receive a 20% raise for the upcoming year. How much more money will Jamie receive next year?
    A. $60,000   B. $10,000   C. $1,000   D. $51,000

22. You and a co-worker work for a temp hiring agency as part of their office staff. You both are given 6 days off per month. How many days off are you and your co-worker given in a year?
    A. 24   B. 72   C. 144   D. 48

23. If Margot makes $34,000 per year and she works 40 hours per week for all 52 weeks, what is her hourly rate?
    A. $16.34/hour   B. $17.00/hour   C. $15.54/hour   D. $13.23/hour

24. How many dimes are there in $175.00?
    A. 175   B. 1,750   C. 3,500   D. 17,500

25. If Janey is three times as old as Emily, and Emily is 3, how old is Janey?
    A. 6   B. 9   C. 12   D. 15

KEY (CORRECT ANSWERS)

1. C
2. D
3. A
4. B
5. B

6. C
7. A
8. B
9. C
10. A

11. B
12. A
13. D
14. B
15. A

16. C
17. A
18. C
19. B
20. A

21. B
22. C
23. A
24. B
25. B

TEST 2

DIRECTIONS: Each question or incomplete statement is followed by several suggested answers or completions. Select the one that BEST answers the question or completes the statement. *PRINT THE LETTER OF THE CORRECT ANSWER IN THE SPACE AT THE RIGHT.*

Questions 1-6.

DIRECTIONS: Questions 1 through 6 are to be answered on the basis of the following information.

item	name of item to be ordered
quantity	minimum number that can be ordered
beginning amount	amount in stock at start of month
amount received	amount receiving during month
ending amount	amount in stock at end of month
amount used	amount used during month
amount to order	will need at least as much of each item as used in the previous month
unit price	cost of each unit of an item
total price	total price for the order

Item	Quantity	Beginning	Received	Ending	Amount Used	Amount to Order	Unit Price	Total Price
Pens	10	22	10	8	24	20	$0.11	$2.20
Spiral notebooks	8	30	13	12			$0.25	
Binder clips	2 boxes	3 boxes	1 box	1 box			$1.79	
Sticky notes	3 packs	12 packs	4 packs	2 packs			$1.29	
Dry erase markers	1 pack (dozen)	34 markers	8 markers	40 markers			$16.49	
Ink cartridges (printer)	1 cartridge	3 cartridges	1 cartridge	2 cartridges			$79.99	
Folders	10 folders	25 folders	15 folders	10 folders			$1.08	

1. How many packs of sticky notes were used during the month?   1.____
   A. 16   B. 10   C. 12   D. 14

2. How many folders need to be ordered for next month?   2.____
   A. 15   B. 20   C. 30   D. 40

3. What is the total price of notebooks that you will need to order?   3.____
   A. $6.00   B. $0.25   C. $4.50   D. $2.75

4. Which of the following will you spend the second most money on?   4.____
   A. Ink cartridges   B. Dry erase markers
   C. Sticky notes   D. Binder clips

5. How many packs of dry erase markers should you order?   5.____
   A. 1   B. 8   C. 12   D. 0

6. What will be the total price of the file folders you order? 6._____
   A. $20.16 B. $21.60 C. $10.80 D. $4.32

Questions 7-11.

DIRECTIONS: Questions 7 through 11 are to be answered on the basis of the following table.

Number of Car Accidents, By Location and Cause, for 2014						
	Location 1		Location 2		Location 3	
Cause	Number	Percent	Number	Percent	Number	Percent
Severe Weather	10		25		30	
Excessive Speeding	20	40	5		10	
Impaired Driving	15		15	25	8	
Miscellaneous	5		15		2	4
TOTALS	50	100	60	100	50	100

7. Which of the following is the third highest cause of accidents for all three locations? 7._____
   A. Severe Weather
   B. Impaired Driving
   C. Miscellaneous
   D. Excessive Speeding

8. The average number of Severe Weather accidents per week at Location 3 for the year (52 weeks) was MOST NEARLY 8._____
   A. 0.57 B. 30 C. 1 D. 1.25

9. Which location had the LARGEST percentage of accidents caused by Impaired Driving? 9._____
   A. 1 B. 2 C. 3 D. Both A and B

10. If one-third of the accidents at all three locations resulted in at least one fatality, what is the LEAST amount of deaths caused by accidents last year? 10._____
    A. 60 B. 106 C. 66 D. 53

11. What is the percentage of accidents caused by miscellaneous means from all three locations in 2014? 11._____
    A. 5% B. 10% C. 13% D. 25%

12. How many pairs of the following groups of letters are exactly alike? 12._____
    ACDOBJ   ACDBOJ
    HEWBWR   HEWRWB
    DEERVS   DEERVS
    BRFQSX   BRFQSX
    WEYRVB   WEYRVB
    SPQRZA   SQRPZA

    A. 2 B. 3 C. 4 D. 5

Questions 13-19.

DIRECTIONS: Questions 13 through 19 are to be answered on the basis of the following information.

In 2012, the most current information on the American population was finished. The information was compiled by 200 volunteers in each of the 50 states. The territory of Puerto Rico, a sovereign of the United States, had 25 people assigned to compile data. In February of 2010, volunteers in each state and sovereign began collecting information. In Puerto Rico, data collection finished by January 31st, 2011, while work in the United States was completed on June 30, 2012. Each volunteer gathered data on the population of their state or sovereign. When the information was compiled, volunteers sent reports to the nation's capital, Washington, D.C. Each volunteer worked 20 hours per month and put together 10 reports per month. After the data was compiled in total, 50 people reviewed the data and worked from January 2012 to December 2012.

13. How many reports were generated from February 2010 to April 2010 in Illinois and Ohio?
    A. 3,000   B. 6,000   C. 12,000   D. 15,000

14. How many volunteers in total collected population data in January 2012?
    A. 10,000   B. 2,000   C. 225   D. 200

15. How many reports were put together in May 2012?
    A. 2,000   B. 50,000   C. 100,000   D. 100,250

16. How many hours did the Puerto Rican volunteers work in the fall (September-November)?
    A. 60   B. 500   C. 1,500   D. 0

17. How many workers were compiling or reviewing data in July 2012?
    A. 25   B. 50   C. 200   D. 250

18. What was the total amount of hours worked by Nevada volunteers in July 2010?
    A. 500   B. 4,000   C. 4,500   D. 5,000

19. How many reviewers worked in January 2013?
    A. 75   B. 50   C. 0   D. 25

20. John has to file 10 documents per shelf. How many documents would it take for John to fill 40 shelves?
    A. 40   B. 400   C. 4,500   D. 5,000

21. Jill wants to travel from New York City to Los Angeles by bike, which is approximately 2,772 miles. How many miles per day would Jill need to average if she wanted to complete the trip in 4 weeks?
    A. 100   B. 89   C. 99   D. 94

4 (#2)

22. If there are 24 CPU's and only 7 monitors, how many more monitors do you need to have the same amount of monitors as CPU's?
    A. Not enough information
    B. 17
    C. 31
    D. 0

    22._____

23. If Gerry works 5 days a week and 8 hours each day, and John works 3 days a week and 10 hours each day, how many more hours per year will Gerry work than John?
    A. They work the same amount of hours.
    B. 450
    C. 520
    D. 832

    23._____

24. Jimmy gets transferred to a new office. The new office has 25 employees, but only 16 are there due to a blizzard. How many coworkers was Jimmy able to meet on his first day?
    A. 16   B. 25   C. 9   D. 7

    24._____

25. If you do a fundraiser for charities in your area and raise $500 total, how much would you give to each charity if you were donating equal amounts to 3 of them?
    A. $250.00   B. $167.77   C. $50.00   D. $111.11

    25._____

KEY (CORRECT ANSWERS)

1.	D		11.	C
2.	B		12.	B
3.	A		13.	C
4.	C		14.	A
5.	D		15.	C
6.	B		16.	C
7.	D		17.	B
8.	A		18.	B
9.	A		19.	C
10.	D		20.	B

21.	C
22.	B
23.	C
24.	A
25.	B

TEST 3

DIRECTIONS: Each question or incomplete statement is followed by several suggested answers or completions. Select the one that BEST answers the question or completes the statement. *PRINT THE LETTER OF THE CORRECT ANSWER IN THE SPACE AT THE RIGHT.*

Questions 1-3.

DIRECTIONS: In answering Questions 1 through 3, choose the correctly spelled word.

1. A. allusion B. alusion C. allusien D. allution 1.____

2. A. altitude B. alltitude C. atlitude D. altlitude 2.____

3. A. althogh B. allthough C. althrough D. although 3.____

Questions 4-9.

DIRECTIONS: In answering Questions 4 through 9, choose the answer that BEST completes the analogy.

4. Odometer is to mileage as compass is to 4.____
   A. speed B. needle C. hiking D. direction

5. Marathon is to race as hibernation is to 5.____
   A. winter B. dream C. sleep D. bear

6. Cup is to coffee as bowl is to 6.____
   A. dish B. spoon C. food D. soup

7. Flow is to river as stagnant is to 7.____
   A. pool B. rain C. stream D. canal

8. Paw is to cat as hoof is to 8.____
   A. lamb B. horse C. lion D. elephant

9. Architect is to building as sculptor is to 9.____
   A. museum B. chisel C. stone D. statue

115

Questions 10-14.

DIRECTIONS: Questions 10 through 14 are to be answered on the basis of the following graph.

Population of Carroll City Broken Down by Age and Gender (in Thousands)			
Age	Female	Male	Total
Under 15	60	60	120
15-23		22	
24-33		20	44
34-43	13	18	31
44-53	20		67
64 and Over	65	65	130
TOTAL	230	232	462

10. How many people in the city are between the ages of 15-23? 10.____
    A. 70   B. 46,000   C. 70,000   D. 225,000

11. Approximately what percentage of the total population of the city was female aged 24-33? 11.____
    A. 10%   B. 5%   C. 15%   D. 25%

12. If 33% of the males have a job and 55% of females don't have a job, which of the following statements is TRUE? 12.____
    A. Males have approximately 2,600 more jobs than females.
    B. Females have approximately 49,000 more jobs than males.
    C. Females have approximately 26,000 more jobs than males.
    D. None of the above statements are true.

13. How many females between the ages of 15-23 live in Carroll City? 13.____
    A. 67,000   B. 24,000   C. 48,000   D. 91,000

14. Assume all males 44-53 living in Carroll City are employed. If two-thirds of males age 44-53 work jobs outside of Carroll City, how many work within city limits? 14.____
    A. 31,333
    B. 15,667
    C. 47,000
    D. Cannot answer the question with the information provided

Questions 15-16.

DIRECTIONS: Questions 15 and 16 are labeled as shown. Alphabetize them for filing. Choose the answer that correctly shows the order.

15. (1) AED
    (2) OOS
    (3) FOA
    (4) DOM
    (5) COB

    A. 2-5-4-3-2   B. 1-4-5-2-3   C. 1-5-4-2-3   D. 1-5-4-3-2

15.____

16. Alphabetize the names of the people. Last names are given last.
    (1) Lindsey Jamestown
    (2) Jane Alberta
    (3) Ally Jamestown
    (4) Allison Johnston
    (5) Lyle Moreno

    A. 2-1-3-4-5   B. 3-4-2-1-5   C. 2-3-1-4-5   D. 4-3-2-1-5

16.____

17. Which of the following words is misspelled?
    A. disgust   B. whisper
    C. locale   D. none of the above

17.____

Questions 18-21.

DIRECTIONS: Questions 18 through 21 are to be answered on the basis of the following list of employees.

        Robertson, Aaron
        Bacon, Gina
        Jerimiah, Trace
        Gillette, Stanley
        Jacks, Sharon

18. Which employee name would come in third in alphabetized list?
    A. Robertson, Aaron   B. Jerimiah, Trace
    C. Gillette, Stanley   D. Jacks, Sharon

18.____

19. Which employee's first name starts with the letter in the alphabet that is five letters after the first letter of their last name?
    A. Jerimiah, Trace   B. Bacon, Gina
    C. Jacks, Sharon   D. Gillette, Stanley

19.____

20. How many employees have last names that are exactly five letters long?
    A. 1   B. 2   C. 3   D. 4

20.____

21. How many of the employees have either a first or last name that starts with the letter "G"?   21.____
    A. 1   B. 2   C. 4   D. 5

Questions 22-25.

DIRECTIONS: Questions 22 through 25 are to be answered on the basis of the following chart.

Bicycle Sales (Model #34JA32)							
Country	May	June	July	August	September	October	Total
Germany	34	47	45	54	56	60	296
Britain	40	44	36	47	47	46	260
Ireland	37	32	32	32	34	33	200
Portugal	14	14	14	16	17	14	89
Italy	29	29	28	31	29	31	177
Belgium	22	24	24	26	25	23	144
Total	176	198	179	206	208	207	1166

22. What percentage of the overall total was sold to the German importer?   22.____
    A. 25.3%   B. 22%   C. 24.1%   D. 23%

23. What percentage of the overall total was sold in September?   23.____
    A. 24.1%   B. 25.6%   C. 17.9%   D. 24.6%

24. What is the average number of units per month imported into Belgium over the first four months shown?   24.____
    A. 26   B. 20   C. 24   D. 31

25. If you look at the three smallest importers, what is their total import percentage?   25.____
    A. 35.1%   B. 37.1%   C. 40%   D. 28%

KEY (CORRECT ANSWERS)

1. A
2. A
3. D
4. D
5. C

6. D
7. A
8. B
9. D
10. C

11. B
12. C
13. C
14. B
15. D

16. C
17. D
18. D
19. B
20. B

21. B
22. A
23. C
24. C
25. A

TEST 4

DIRECTIONS: Each question or incomplete statement is followed by several suggested answers or completions. Select the one that BEST answers the question or completes the statement. *PRINT THE LETTER OF THE CORRECT ANSWER IN THE SPACE AT THE RIGHT.*

Questions 1-6.

DIRECTIONS: In answering Questions 1 through 6, choose the sentence that represents the BEST example of English grammar.

1.
   A. Joey and me want to go on a vacation next week.
   B. Gary told Jim he would need to take some time off.
   C. If turning six years old, Jim's uncle would teach Spanish to him.
   D. Fax a copy of your resume to Ms. Perez and me.

   1.____

2.
   A. Jerry stood in line for almost two hours.
   B. The reaction to my engagement was less exciting than I thought it would be.
   C. Carlos and me have done great work on this project.
   D. Two parts of the speech needs to be revised before tomorrow.

   2.____

3.
   A. Arriving home, the alarm was tripped.
   B. Jonny is regarded as a stand up guy, a responsible parent, and he doesn't give up until a task is finished.
   C. Each employee must submit a drug test each month.
   D. One of the documents was incinerated in the explosion.

   3.____

4.
   A. As soon as my parents get home, I told them I finished all of my chores.
   B. I asked my teacher to send me my missing work, check my absences, and how did I do on my test.
   C. Matt attempted to keep it concealed from Jenny and me.
   D. If Mary or him cannot get work done on time, I will have to split them up.

   4.____

5.
   A. Driving to work, the traffic report warned him of an accident on Highway 47.
   B. Jimmy has performed well this season.
   C. Since finishing her degree, several job offers have been given to Cam.
   D. Our boss is creating unstable conditions for we employees.

   5.____

6.
   A. The thief was described as a tall man with a wiry mustache weighing approximately 150 pounds.
   B. She gave Patrick and I some more time to finish our work.
   C. One of the books that he ordered was damaged in shipping.
   D. While talking on the rotary phone, the car Jim was driving skidded off the road.

   6.____

Questions 7-9.

DIRECTIONS: Questions 7 through 9 are to be answered on the basis of the following graph.

Ice Lake Frozen Flight (2002-2013)		
Year	Number of Participants	Temperature (Fahrenheit)
2002	22	4°
2003	50	33°
2004	69	18°
2005	104	22°
2006	108	24°
2007	288	33°
2008	173	9°
2009	598	39°
2010	698	26°
2011	696	30°
2012	777	28°
2013	578	32°

7. Which two year span had the LARGEST difference between temperatures?
   A. 2002 and 2003
   B. 2011 and 2012
   C. 2008 and 2009
   D. 2003 and 2004

8. How many total people participated in the years after the temperature reached at least 29°?
   A. 2,295   B. 1,717   C. 2,210   D. 4,543

9. In 2007, the event saw 288 participants, while in 2008 that number dropped to 173. Which of the following reasons BEST explains the drop in participants?
   A. The event had not been going on that long and people didn't know about it.
   B. The lake water wasn't cold enough to have people jump in.
   C. The temperature was too cold for many people who would have normally participated.
   D. None of the above reasons explain the drop in participants.

10. In the following list of numbers, how many times does 4 come just after 2 when 2 comes just after an odd number?
    2365247653898632488572486392424
    A. 2   B. 3   C. 4   D. 5

11. Which choice below lists the letter that is as far after B as S is after N in the alphabet?
    A. G   B. H   C. I   D. J

Questions 12-15.

DIRECTIONS: Questions 12 through 15 are to be answered on the basis of the following directory and list of changes.

Directory		
Name	Emp. Type	Position
Julie Taylor	Warehouse	Packer
James King	Office	Administrative Assistant
John Williams	Office	Salesperson
Ray Moore	Warehouse	Maintenance
Kathleen Byrne	Warehouse	Supervisor
Amy Jones	Office	Salesperson
Paul Jonas	Office	Salesperson
Lisa Wong	Warehouse	Loader
Eugene Lee	Office	Accountant
Bruce Lavine	Office	Manager
Adam Gates	Warehouse	Packer
Will Suter	Warehouse	Packer
Gary Lorper	Office	Accountant
Jon Adams	Office	Salesperson
Susannah Harper	Office	Salesperson

Directory Updates:
- Employee e-mail addresses will adhere to the following guidelines: lastnamefirstname@apexindustries.com (ex. Susannah Harper is harpersusannah@apexindustries.com). Currently, employees in the warehouse share one e-mail, distribution@apexindustries.com.
- The "Loader" position will now be referred to as "Specialist I"
- Adam Gates has accepted a Supervisor position within the Warehouse and is no longer a Packer. All warehouse employees report to the two Supervisors and all office employees report to the Manager.

12. Amy Jones tried to send an e-mail to Adam Gates, but it wouldn't send. Which of the following offers the BEST explanation?
    A. Amy put Adam's first name first and then his last name.
    B. Adam doesn't check his e-mail, so he wouldn't know if he received the e-mail or not.
    C. Adam does not have his own e-mail.
    D. Office employees are not allowed to send e-mails to each other.

13. How many Packers currently work for Apex Industries?
    A. 2   B. 3   C. 4   D. 5

14. What position does Lisa Wong currently hold?
    A. Specialist I
    B. Secretary
    C. Administrative Assistant
    D. Loader

15. If an employee wanted to contact the office manager, which of the following e-mails should the e-mail be sent to?   15.____
    A. officemanager@apexindustries.com
    B. brucelavine@apexindustries.com
    C. lavinebruce@apexindustries.com
    D. distribution@apexindustries.com

Questions 16-19.

DIRECTIONS: In answering Questions 16 through 19, compare the three names, numbers or addresses.

16. Smiley Yarnell   Smiley Yarnel   Smily Yarnell   16.____
    A. All three are exactly alike.
    B. The first and second are exactly alike.
    C. The second and third are exactly alike.
    D. All three are different.

17. 1583 Theater Drive   1583 Theater Drive   1583 Theatre Drive   17.____
    A. All three are exactly alike.
    B. The first and second are exactly alike.
    C. The second and third are exactly alike.
    D. All three are different.

18. 3341893212   3341893212   3341893212   18.____
    A. All three are exactly alike.
    B. The first and second are exactly alike.
    C. The second and third are exactly alike.
    D. All three are different.

19. Douglass Watkins   Douglas Watkins   Douglass Watkins   19.____
    A. All three are exactly alike.
    B. The first and third are exactly alike.
    C. The second and third are exactly alike.
    D. All three are different.

Questions 20-24.

DIRECTIONS: In answering Questions 20 through 24, you will be presented with a word. Choose the synonym that BEST represents the word in question.

20. Flexible   20.____
    A. delicate   B. inflammable   C. strong   D. pliable

21. Alternative   21.____
    A. choice   B. moderate   C. lazy   D. value

22. Corroborate
    A. examine   B. explain   C. verify   D. explain

23. Respiration
    A. recovery   B. breathing   C. sweating   D. selfish

24. Negligent
    A. lazy   B. moderate   C. hopeless   D. lax

25. Plumber is to Wrench as Painter is to
    A. pipe   B. shop   C. hammer   D. brush

KEY (CORRECT ANSWERS)

1. D
2. A
3. D
4. C
5. B

6. C
7. C
8. B
9. C
10. C

11. A
12. C
13. A
14. A
15. C

16. D
17. B
18. A
19. B
20. D

21. A
22. C
23. B
24. D
25. D

PHILOSOPHY, PRINCIPLES, PRACTICES, AND TECHNICS OF SUPERVISION, ADMINISTRATION, MANAGEMENT, AND ORGANIZATION

TABLE OF CONTENTS

	Page
MEANING OF SUPERVISION	1
THE OLD AND THE NEW SUPERVISION	1
THE EIGHT (8) BASIC PRINCIPLES OF THE NEW SUPERVISION	1
I. Principle of Responsibility	1
II. Principle of Authority	2
III. Principle of Self-Growth	2
IV. Principle of Individual Worth	2
V. Principle of Creative Leadership	2
VI. Principle of Success and Failure	2
VII. Principle of Science	3
VIII. Principle of Cooperation	3
WHAT IS ADMINISTRATION?	3
I. Practices Commonly Classed as "Supervisory"	3
II. Practices Commonly Classed as "Administrative"	3
III. Practices Commonly Classed as Both "Supervisory" and "Administrative"	4
RESPONSIBILITIES OF THE SUPERVISOR	4
COMPETENCIES OF THE SUPERVISOR	4
THE PROFESSIONAL SUPERVISOR-EMPLOYEE RELATIONSHIP	4
MINI-TEXT IN SUPERVISION, ADMINISTRATION, MANAGEMENT, AND ORGANIZATION	5
I. Brief Highlights	5
A. Levels of Management	6
B. What the Supervisor Must Learn	6
C. A Definition of Supervision	6
D. Elements of the Team Concept	6
E. Principles of Organization	6
F. The Four Important Parts of Every Job	7
G. Principles of Delegation	7
H. Principles of Effective Communications	7
I. Principles of Work Improvement	7
J. Areas of Job Improvement	7
K. Seven Key Points in Making Improvements	8

	L.	Corrective Techniques for Job Improvement	8
	M.	A Planning Checklist	8
	N.	Five Characteristics of Good Directions	9
	O.	Types of Directions	9
	P.	Controls	9
	Q.	Orienting the New Employee	9
	R.	Checklist for Orienting New Employees	9
	S.	Principles of Learning	10
	T.	Causes of Poor Performance	10
	U.	Four Major Steps in On-the-Job Instructions	10
	V.	Employees Want Five Things	10
	W.	Some Don'ts in Regard to Praise	11
	X.	How to Gain Your Workers' Confidence	11
	Y.	Sources of Employee Problems	11
	Z.	The Supervisor's Key to Discipline	11
	AA.	Five Important Processes of Management	12
	BB.	When the Supervisor Fails to Plan	12
	CC.	Fourteen General Principles of Management	12
	DD.	Change	12
II.	Brief Topical Summaries		13
	A.	Who/What is the Supervisor?	13
	B.	The Sociology of Work	13
	C.	Principles and Practices of Supervision	14
	D.	Dynamic Leadership	14
	E.	Processes for Solving Problems	15
	F.	Training for Results	15
	G.	Health, Safety, and Accident Prevention	16
	H.	Equal Employment Opportunity	16
	I.	Improving Communications	16
	J.	Self-Development	17
	K.	Teaching and Training	17
		1. The Teaching Process	17
		a. Preparation	17
		b. Presentation	18
		c. Summary	18
		d. Application	18
		e. Evaluation	18
		2. Teaching Methods	18
		a. Lecture	18
		b. Discussion	18
		c. Demonstration	19
		d. Performance	19
		e. Which Method to Use	19

PHILOSOPHY, PRINCIPLES, PRACTICES, AND TECHNICS
OF
SUPERVISION, ADMINISTRATION, MANAGEMENT, AND ORGANIZATION

MEANING OF SUPERVISION

The extension of the democratic philosophy has been accompanied by an extension in the scope of supervision. Modern leaders and supervisors no longer think of supervision in the narrow sense of being confined chiefly to visiting employees, supplying materials, or rating the staff. They regard supervision as being intimately related to all the concerned agencies of society, they speak of the supervisor's function in terms of "growth," rather than the "improvement" of employees.

This modern concept of supervision may be defined as follows: Supervision is leadership and the development of leadership within groups which are cooperatively engaged in inspection, research, training, guidance, and evaluation.

THE OLD AND THE NEW SUPERVISION

TRADITIONAL
1. Inspection
2. Focused on the employee
3. Visitation
4. Random and haphazard
5. Imposed and authoritarian
6. One person usually

MODERN
1. Study and analysis
2. Focused on aims, materials, methods, supervisors, employees, environment
3. Demonstrations, intervisitation, workshops, directed reading, bulletins, etc.
4. Definitely organized and planned (scientific)
5. Cooperative and democratic
6. Many persons involved (creative)

THE EIGHT (8) BASIC PRINCIPLES OF THE NEW SUPERVISION

I. Principle of Responsibility
   Authority to act and responsibility for acting must be joined.
   A. If you give responsibility, give authority.
   B. Define employee duties clearly.
   C. Protect employees from criticism by others.
   D. Recognize the rights as well as obligations of employees.
   E. Achieve the aims of a democratic society insofar as it is possible within the area of your work.
   F. Establish a situation favorable to training and learning.
   G. Accept ultimate responsibility for everything done in your section, unit, office, division, department.
   H. Good administration and good supervision are inseparable.

II. Principle of Authority
The success of the supervisor is measured by the extent to which the power of authority is not used.
   A. Exercise simplicity and informality in supervision
   B. Use the simplest machinery of supervision
   C. If it is good for the organization as a whole, it is probably justified.
   D. Seldom be arbitrary or authoritative.
   E. Do not base your work on the power of position or of personality.
   F. Permit and encourage the free expression of opinions.

III. Principle of Self-Growth
The success of the supervisor is measured by the extent to which, and the speed with which, he is no longer needed.
   A. Base criticism on principles, not on specifics.
   B. Point out higher activities to employees.
   C. Train for self-thinking by employees to meet new situations.
   D. Stimulate initiative, self-reliance, and individual responsibility
   E. Concentrate on stimulating the growth of employees rather than on removing defects.

IV. Principle of Individual Worth
Respect for the individual is a paramount consideration in supervision.
   A. Be human and sympathetic in dealing with employees.
   B. Don't nag about things to be done.
   C. Recognize the individual differences among employees and seek opportunities to permit best expression of each personality.

V. Principle of Creative Leadership
The best supervision is that which is not apparent to the employee.
   A. Stimulate, don't drive employees to creative action.
   B. Emphasize doing good things.
   C. Encourage employees to do what they do best.
   D. Do not be too greatly concerned with details of subject or method.
   E. Do not be concerned exclusively with immediate problems and activities.
   F. Reveal higher activities and make them both desired and maximally possible.
   G. Determine procedures in the light of each situation but see that these are derived from a sound basic philosophy.
   H. Aid, inspire, and lead so as to liberate the creative spirit latent in all good employees.

VI. Principle of Success and Failure
There are no unsuccessful employees, only unsuccessful supervisors who have failed to give proper leadership.
   A. Adapt suggestions to the capacities, attitudes, and prejudices of employees.
   B. Be gradual, be progressive, be persistent.
   C. Help the employee find the general principle; have the employee apply his own problem to the general principle.
   D. Give adequate appreciation for good work and honest effort.
   E. Anticipate employee difficulties and help to prevent them.
   F. Encourage employees to do the desirable things they will do anyway.
   G. Judge your supervision by the results it secures.

VII. Principle of Science
Successful supervision is scientific, objective, and experimental. It is based on facts, not on prejudices.
   A. Be cumulative in results.
   B. Never divorce your suggestions from the goals of training.
   C. Don't be impatient of results.
   D. Keep all matters on a professional, not a personal, level.
   E. Do not be concerned exclusively with immediate problems and activities.
   F. Use objective means of determining achievement and rating where possible.

VIII. Principle of Cooperation
Supervision is a cooperative enterprise between supervisor and employee.
   A. Begin with conditions as they are.
   B. Ask opinions of all involved when formulating policies.
   C. Organization is as good as its weakest link.
   D. Let employees help to determine policies and department programs.
   E. Be approachable and accessible—physically and mentally.
   F. Develop pleasant social relationships.

WHAT IS ADMINISTRATION

Administration is concerned with providing the environment, the material facilities, and the operational procedures that will promote the maximum growth and development of supervisors and employees. (Organization is an aspect and a concomitant of administration.)

There is no sharp line of demarcation between supervision and administration; these functions are intimately interrelated and, often, overlapping. They are complementary activities.

I. Practices Commonly Classed as "Supervisory"
   A. Conducting employees' conferences
   B. Visiting sections, units, offices, divisions, departments
   C. Arranging for demonstrations
   D. Examining plans
   E. Suggesting professional reading
   F. Interpreting bulletins
   G. Recommending in-service training courses
   H. Encouraging experimentation
   I. Appraising employee morale
   J. Providing for intervisitation

II. Practices Commonly Classified as "Administrative"
   A. Management of the office
   B. Arrangement of schedules for extra duties
   C. Assignment of rooms or areas
   D. Distribution of supplies
   E. Keeping records and reports
   F. Care of audio-visual materials
   G. Keeping inventory records
   H. Checking record cards and books

4

  I. Programming special activities
  J. Checking on the attendance and punctuality of employees

III. Practices Commonly Classified as Both "Supervisory" and "Administrative"
  A. Program construction
  B. Testing or evaluating outcomes
  C. Personnel accounting
  D. Ordering instructional materials

RESPONSIBILITIES OF THE SUPERVISOR

A person employed in a supervisory capacity must constantly be able to improve his own efficiency and ability. He represent the employer to the employees and only continuous self-examination can make him a capable supervisor.

Leadership and training are the supervisor's responsibility. An efficient working unit is one in which the employees work with the supervisor. It is his job to bring out the best in his employees. He must always be relaxed, courteous, and calm in his association with his employees. Their feelings are important, and a harsh attitude does not develop the most efficient employees.

COMPETENCES OF THE SUPERVISOR

  I. Complete knowledge of the duties and responsibilities of his position.
  II. To be able to organize a job, plan ahead, and carry through.
  III. To have self-confidence and initiative.
  IV. To be able to handle the unexpected situation and make quick decisions.
  V. To be able to properly train subordinates in the positions they are best suited for.
  VI. To be able to keep good human relations among his subordinates.
  VII. To be able to keep good human relations between his subordinates and himself and to earn their respect and trust.

THE PROFESSIONAL SUPERVISOR-EMPLOYEE RELATIONSHIP

There are two kinds of efficiency: one kind is only apparent and is produced in organizations through the exercise of mere discipline; this is but a simulation of the second, or true, efficiency which springs from spontaneous cooperation. If you are a manager, no matter how great or small your responsibility, it is your job, in the final analysis, to create and develop this involuntary cooperation among the people whom you supervise. For, no matter how powerful a combination of money, machines, and materials a company may have, this is a dead and sterile thing without a team of willing, thinking, and articulate people to guide it.

The following 21 points are presented as indicative of the exemplary basic relationship that should exist between supervisor and employee:

1. Each person wants to be liked and respected by his fellow employee and wants to be treated with consideration and respect by his superior.
2. The most competent employee will make an error. However, in a unit where good relations exist between the supervisor and his employees, tenseness and fear do not exist. Thus, errors are not hidden or covered up, and the efficiency of a unit is not impaired.

3. Subordinates resent rules, regulations, or orders that are unreasonable or unexplained.
4. Subordinates are quick to resent unfairness, harshness, injustices, and favoritism.
5. An employee will accept responsibility if he knows that he will be complimented for a job well done, and not too harshly chastised for failure; that his supervisor will check the cause of the failure, and, if it was the supervisor's fault, he will assume the blame therefore. If it was the employee's fault, his supervisor will explain the correct method or means of handling the responsibility.
6. An employee wants to receive credit for a suggestion he has made, that is used. If a suggestion cannot be used, the employee is entitled to an explanation. The supervisor should not say "no" and close the subject.
7. Fear and worry slow up a worker's ability. Poor working environment can impair his physical and mental health. A good supervisor avoids forceful methods, threats, and arguments to get a job done.
8. A forceful supervisor is able to train his employees individually and as a team, and is able to motivate them in the proper channels.
9. A mature supervisor is able to properly evaluate his subordinates and to keep them happy and satisfied.
10. A sensitive supervisor will never patronize his subordinates.
11. A worthy supervisor will respect his employees' confidences.
12. Definite and clear-cut responsibilities should be assigned to each executive.
13. Responsibility should always be coupled with corresponding authority.
14. No change should be made in the scope or responsibilities of a position without a definite understanding to that effect on the part of all persons concerned.
15. No executive or employee, occupying a single position in the organization, should be subject to definite orders from more than one source.
16. Orders should never be given to subordinates over the head of a responsible executive. Rather than do this, the officer in question should be supplanted.
17. Criticisms of subordinates should, whoever possible, be made privately, and in no case should a subordinate be criticized in the presence of executives or employees of equal or lower rank.
18. No dispute or difference between executives or employees as to authority or responsibilities should be considered too trivial for prompt and careful adjudication.
19. Promotions, wage changes, and disciplinary action should always be approved by the executive immediately superior to the one directly responsible.
20. No executive or employee should ever be required, or expected, to be at the same time an assistant to, and critic of, another.
21. Any executive whose work is subject to regular inspection should, wherever practicable, be given the assistance and facilities necessary to enable him to maintain an independent check of the quality of his work.

MINI-TEXT IN SUPERVISION, ADMINISTRATION, MANAGEMENT, AND ORGANIZATION

I. Brief Highlights

   Listed concisely and sequentially are major headings and important data in the field for quick recall and review.

A. Levels of Management
Any organization of some size has several levels of management. In terms of a ladder, the levels are:

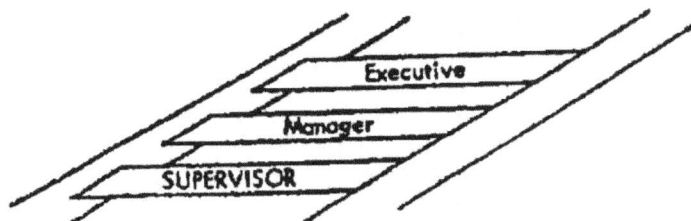

The first level is very important because it is the beginning point of management leadership.

B. What the Supervisor Must Learn
A supervisor must learn to:
1. Deal with people and their differences
2. Get the job done through people
3. Recognize the problems when they exist
4. Overcome obstacles to good performance
5. Evaluate the performance of people
6. Check his own performance in terms of accomplishment

C. A Definition of Supervisor
The term supervisor means any individual having authority, in the interests of the employer, to hire, transfer, suspend, lay-off, recall, promote, discharge, assign, reward, or discipline other employees or responsibility to direct them, or to adjust their grievances, or effectively to recommend such action, if, in connection with the foregoing, exercise of such authority is not of a merely routine or clerical nature but requires the use of independent judgment.

D. Elements of the Team Concept
What is involved in teamwork? The component parts are:
1. Members
2. A leader
3. Goals
4. Plans
5. Cooperation
6. Spirit

E. Principles of Organization
1. A team member must know what his job is.
2. Be sure that the nature and scope of a job are understood.
3. Authority and responsibility should be carefully spelled out.
4. A supervisor should be permitted to make the maximum number of decisions affecting his employees.
5. Employees should report to only one supervisor.
6. A supervisor should direct only as many employees as he can handle effectively.
7. An organization plan should be flexible.

8. Inspection and performance of work should be separate.
9. Organizational problems should receive immediate attention.
10. Assign work in line with ability and experience.

F. The Four Important Parts of Every Job
1. Inherent in every job is the *accountability* for results.
2. A second set of factors in every job is *responsibilities*.
3. Along with duties and responsibilities one must have the *authority* to act within certain limits without obtaining permission to proceed.
4. No job exists in a vacuum. The supervisor is surrounded by key *relationships*.

G. Principles of Delegation
Where work is delegated for the first time, the supervisor should think in terms of these questions:
1. Who is best qualified to do this?
2. Can an employee improve his abilities by doing this?
3. How long should an employee spend on this?
4. Are there any special problems for which he will need guidance?
5. How broad a delegation can I make?

H. Principles of Effective Communications
1. Determine the media.
2. To whom directed?
3. Identification and source authority.
4. Is communication understood?

I. Principles of Work Improvement
1. Most people usually do only the work which is assigned to them.
2. Workers are likely to fit assigned work into the time available to perform it.
3. A good workload usually stimulates output.
4. People usually do their best work when they know that results will be reviewed or inspected.
5. Employees usually feel that someone else is responsible for conditions of work, workplace layout, job methods, type of tools/equipment, and other such factors.
6. Employees are usually defensive about their job security.
7. Employees have natural resistance to change.
8. Employees can support or destroy a supervisor.
9. A supervisor usually earns the respect of his people through his personal example of diligence and efficiency.

J. Areas of Job Improvement
The areas of job improvement are quite numerous, but the most common ones which a supervisor can identify and utilize are:
1. Departmental layout
2. Flow of work
3. Workplace layout
4. Utilization of manpower
5. Work methods
6. Materials handling

7. Utilization
8. Motion economy

K. Seven Key Points in Making Improvements
1. Select the job to be improved
2. Study how it is being done now
3. Question the present method
4. Determine actions to be taken
5. Chart proposed method
6. Get approval and apply
7. Solicit worker participation

l. Corrective Techniques of Job Improvement
Specific Problems
1. Size of workload
2. Inability to meet schedules
3. Strain and fatigue
4. Improper use of men and skills
5. Waste, poor quality, unsafe conditions
6. Bottleneck conditions that hinder output
7. Poor utilization of equipment and machine
8. Efficiency and productivity of labor

General Improvement
1. Departmental layout
2. Flow of work
3. Work plan layout
4. Utilization of manpower
5. Work methods
6. Materials handling
7. Utilization of equipment
8. Motion economy

Corrective Techniques
1. Study with scale model
2. Flow chart study
3. Motion analysis
4. Comparison of units produced to standard allowance
5. Methods analysis
6. Flow chart and equipment study
7. Down time vs. running time
8. Motion analysis

M. A Planning Checklist
1. Objectives
2. Controls
3. Delegations
4. Communications
5. Resources
6. Manpower

7. Equipment
8. Supplies and materials
9. Utilization of time
10. Safety
11. Money
12. Work
13. Timing of improvements

N. Five Characteristics of Good Directions
In order to get results, directions must be:
1. Possible of accomplishment
2. Agreeable with worker interests
3. Related to mission
4. Planned and complete
5. Unmistakably clear

O. Types of Directions
1. Demands or direct orders
2. Requests
3. Suggestion or implication
4. volunteering

P. Controls
A typical listing of the overall areas in which the supervisor should establish controls might be:
1. Manpower
2. Materials
3. Quality of work
4. Quantity of work
5. Time
6. Space
7. Money
8. Methods

Q. Orienting the New Employee
1. Prepare for him
2. Welcome the new employee
3. Orientation for the job
4. Follow-up

R. Checklist for Orienting New Employees   Yes   No
1. Do you appreciate the feelings of new employees when they first report for work?   ___ ___
2. Are you aware of the fact that the new employee must make a big adjustment to his job?   ___ ___
3. Have you given him good reasons for liking the job and the organization?   ___ ___
4. Have you prepared for his first day on the job?   ___ ___
5. Did you welcome him cordially and make him feel needed?   ___ ___

	Yes	No

6. Did you establish rapport with him so that he feels free to talk and discuss matters with you? ___ ___
7. Did you explain his job to him and his relationship to you? ___ ___
8. Does he know that his work will be evaluated periodically on a basis that is fair and objective? ___ ___
9. Did you introduce him to his fellow workers in such a way that they are likely to accept him? ___ ___
10. Does he know what employee benefits he will receive? ___ ___
11. Does he understand the importance of being on the job and what to do if he must leave his duty station? ___ ___
12. Has he been impressed with the importance of accident prevention and safe practice? ___ ___
13. Does he generally know his way around the department? ___ ___
14. Is he under the guidance of a sponsor who will teach the right way of doing things? ___ ___
15. Do you plan to follow-up so that he will continue to adjust successfully to his job? ___ ___

S. Principles of Learning
1. Motivation
2. Demonstration or explanation
3. Practice

T. Causes of Poor Performance
1. Improper training for job
2. Wrong tools
3. Inadequate directions
4. Lack of supervisory follow-up
5. Poor communications
6. Lack of standards of performance
7. Wrong work habits
8. Low morale
9. Other

U. Four Major Steps in On-The-Job Instruction
1. Prepare the worker
2. Present the operation
3. Tryout performance
4. Follow-up

V. Employees Want Five Things
1. Security
2. Opportunity
3. Recognition
4. Inclusion
5. Expression

W. Some Don'ts in Regard to Praise
1. Don't praise a person for something he hasn't done.
2. Don't praise a person unless you can be sincere.
3. Don't be sparing in praise just because your superior withholds it from you.
4. Don't let too much time elapse between good performance and recognition of it

X. How to Gain Your Workers' Confidence
Methods of developing confidence include such things as:
1. Knowing the interests, habits, hobbies of employees
2. Admitting your own inadequacies
3. Sharing and telling of confidence in others
4. Supporting people when they are in trouble
5. Delegating matters that can be well handled
6. Being frank and straightforward about problems and working conditions
7. Encouraging others to bring their problems to you
8. Taking action on problems which impede worker progress

Y. Sources of Employee Problems
On-the-job causes might be such things as:
1. A feeling that favoritism is exercised in assignments
2. Assignment of overtime
3. An undue amount of supervision
4. Changing methods or systems
5. Stealing of ideas or trade secrets
6. Lack of interest in job
7. Threat of reduction in force
8. Ignorance or lack of communications
9. Poor equipment
10. Lack of knowing how supervisor feels toward employee
11. Shift assignments

Off-the-job problems might have to do with:
1. Health
2. Finances
3. Housing
4. Family

Z. The Supervisor's Key to Discipline
There are several key points about discipline which the supervisor should keep in mind:
1. Job discipline is one of the disciplines of life and is directed by the supervisor.
2. It is more important to correct an employee fault than to fix blame for it.
3. Employee performance is affected by problems both on the job and off.
4. Sudden or abrupt changes in behavior can be indications of important employee problems.
5. Problems should be dealt with as soon as possible after they are identified.
6. The attitude of the supervisor may have more to do with solving problems than the techniques of problem solving.
7. Correction of employee behavior should be resorted to only after the supervisor is sure that training or counseling will not be helpful.

8. Be sure to document your disciplinary actions.
9. Make sure that you are disciplining on the basis of facts rather than personal feelings.
10. Take each disciplinary step in order, being careful not to make snap judgments, or decisions based on impatience.

AA. Five Important Processes of Management
1. Planning
2. Organizing
3. Scheduling
4. Controlling
5. Motivating

BB. When the Supervisor Fails to Plan
1. Supervisor creates impression of not knowing his job
2. May lead to excessive overtime
3. Job runs itself—supervisor lacks control
4. Deadlines and appointments missed
5. Parts of the work go undone
6. Work interrupted by emergencies
7. Sets a bad example
8. Uneven workload creates peaks and valleys
9. Too much time on minor details at expense of more important tasks

CC. Fourteen General Principles of Management
1. Division of work
2. Authority and responsibility
3. Discipline
4. Unity of command
5. Unity of direction
6. Subordination of individual interest to general interest
7. Remuneration of personnel
8. Centralization
9. Scalar chain
10. Order
11. Equity
12. Stability of tenure of personnel
13. Initiative
14. Esprit de corps

DD. Change

Bringing about change is perhaps attempted more often, and yet less well understood, than anything else the supervisor does. How do people generally react to change? (People tend to resist change that is imposed upon them by other individuals or circumstances.

Change is characteristic of every situation. It is a part of every real endeavor where the efforts of people are concerned.

1. Why do people resist change?
   People may resist change because of:
   a. Fear of the unknown
   b. Implied criticism
   c. Unpleasant experiences in the past
   d. Fear of loss of status
   e. Threat to the ego
   f. Fear of loss of economic stability

2. How can we best overcome the resistance to change?
   In initiating change, take these steps:
   a. Get ready to sell
   b. Identify sources of help
   c. Anticipate objections
   d. Sell benefits
   e. Listen in depth
   f. Follow up

II. Brief Topical Summaries

   A. Who/What is the Supervisor?
      1. The supervisor is often called the "highest level employee and the lowest level manager."
      2. A supervisor is a member of both management and the work group. He acts as a bridge between the two.
      3. Most problems in supervision are in the area of human relations, or people problems.
      4. Employees expect: Respect, opportunity to learn and to advance, and a sense of belonging, and so forth.
      5. Supervisors are responsible for directing people and organizing work. Planning is of paramount importance.
      6. A position description is a set of duties and responsibilities inherent to a given position.
      7. It is important to keep the position description up-to-date and to provide each employee with his own copy.

   B. The Sociology of Work
      1. People are alike in many ways; however, each individual is unique.
      2. The supervisor is challenged in getting to know employee differences. Acquiring skills in evaluating individuals is an asset.
      3. Maintaining meaningful working relationships in the organization is of great importance.
      4. The supervisor has an obligation to help individuals to develop to their fullest potential.
      5. Job rotation on a planned basis helps to build versatility and to maintain interest and enthusiasm in work groups.
      6. Cross training (job rotation) provides backup skills.

7. The supervisor can help reduce tension by maintaining a sense of humor, providing guidance to employees, and by making reasonable and timely decisions. Employees respond favorably to working under reasonably predictable circumstances.
8. Change is characteristic of all managerial behavior. The supervisor must adjust to changes in procedures, new methods, technological changes, and to a number of new and sometimes challenging situations.
9. To overcome the natural tendency for people to resist change, the supervisor should become more skillful in initiating change.

C. Principles and Practices of Supervision
1. Employees should be required to answer to only one superior.
2. A supervisor can effectively direct only a limited number of employees, depending upon the complexity, variety, and proximity of the jobs involved.
3. The organizational chart presents the organization in graphic form. It reflects lines of authority and responsibility as well as interrelationships of units within the organization.
4. Distribution of work can be improved through an analysis using the "Work Distribution Chart."
5. The "Work Distribution Chart" reflects the division of work within a unit in understandable form.
6. When related tasks are given to an employee, he has a better chance of increasing his skills through training.
7. The individual who is given the responsibility for tasks must also be given the appropriate authority to insure adequate results.
8. The supervisor should delegate repetitive, routine work. Preparation of recurring reports, maintaining leave and attendance records are some examples.
9. Good discipline is essential to good task performance. Discipline is reflected in the actions of employees on the job in the absence of supervision.
10. Disciplinary action may have to be taken when the positive aspects of discipline have failed. Reprimand, warning, and suspension are examples of disciplinary action.
11. If a situation calls for a reprimand, be sure it is deserved and remember it is to be done in private.

D. Dynamic Leadership
1. A style is a personal method or manner of exerting influence.
2. Authoritarian leaders often see themselves as the source of power and authority.
3. The democratic leader often perceives the group as the source of authority and power.
4. Supervisors tend to do better when using the pattern of leadership that is most natural for them.
5. Social scientists suggest that the effective supervisor use the leadership style that best fits the problem or circumstances involved.
6. All four styles—telling, selling, consulting, joining—have their place. Using one does not preclude using the other at another time.

7. The theory X point of view assumes that the average person dislikes work, will avoid it whenever possible, and must be coerced to achieve organizational objectives.
8. The theory Y point of view assumes that the average person considers work to be a natural as play, and, when the individual is committed, he requires little supervision or direction to accomplish desired objectives.
9. The leader's basic assumptions concerning human behavior and human nature affect his actions, decisions, and other managerial practices.
10. Dissatisfaction among employees is often present, but difficult to isolate. The supervisor should seek to weaken dissatisfaction by keeping promises, being sincere and considerate, keeping employees informed, and so forth.
11. Constructive suggestions should be encouraged during the natural progress of the work.

E. Processes for Solving Problems
1. People find their daily tasks more meaningful and satisfying when they can improve them.
2. The causes of problems, or the key factors, are often hidden in the background. Ability to solve problems often involves the ability to isolate them from their backgrounds. There is some substance to the cliché that some persons "can't see the forest for the trees."
3. New procedures are often developed from old ones. Problems should be broken down into manageable parts. New ideas can be adapted from old one.
4. People think differently in problem-solving situations. Using a logical, patterned approach is often useful. One approach found to be useful includes these steps:
   a. Define the problem
   b. Establish objectives
   c. Get the facts
   d. Weigh and decide
   e. Take action
   f. Evaluate action

F. Training for Results
1. Participants respond best when they feel training is important to them.
2. The supervisor has responsibility for the training and development of those who report to him.
3. When training is delegated to others, great care must be exercised to insure the trainer has knowledge, aptitude, and interest for his work as a trainer.
4. Training (learning) of some type goes on continually. The most successful supervisor makes certain the learning contributes in a productive manner to operational goals.
5. New employees are particularly susceptible to training. Older employees facing new job situations require specific training, as well as having need for development and growth opportunities.
6. Training needs require continuous monitoring.
7. The training officer of an agency is a professional with a responsibility to assist supervisors in solving training problems.

8. Many of the self-development steps important to the supervisor's own growth are equally important to the development of peers and subordinates. Knowledge of these is important when the supervisor consults with others on development and growth opportunities.

G. Health, Safety, and Accident Prevention
1. Management-minded supervisors take appropriate measures to assist employees in maintaining health and in assuring safe practices in the work environment.
2. Effective safety training and practices help to avoid injury and accidents.
3. Safety should be a management goal. All infractions of safety which are observed should be corrected without exception.
4. Employees' safety attitude, training and instruction, provision of safe tools and equipment, supervision, and leadership are considered highly important factors which contribute to safety and which can be influenced directly by supervisors.
5. When accidents do occur, they should be investigated promptly for very important reasons, including the fact that information which is gained can be used to prevent accidents in the future.

H. Equal Employment Opportunity
1. The supervisor should endeavor to treat all employees fairly, without regard to religion, race, sex, or national origin.
2. Groups tend to reflect the attitude of the leader. Prejudice can be detected even in very subtle form. Supervisors must strive to create a feeling of mutual respect and confidence in every employee.
3. Complete utilization of all human resources is a national goal. Equitable consideration should be accorded women in the work force, minority-group members, the physically and mentally handicapped, and the older employee. The important question is: "Who can do the job?"
4. Training opportunities, recognition for performance, overtime assignments, promotional opportunities, and all other personnel actions are to be handled on an equitable basis.

I. Improving Communications
1. Communications is achieving understanding between the sender and the receiver of a message. It also means sharing information—the creation of understanding.
2. Communication is basic to all human activity. Words are means of conveying meanings; however, real meanings are in people.
3. There are very practical differences in the effectiveness of one-way, impersonal, and two-way communications. Words spoken face-to-face are better understood. Telephone conversations are effective, but lack the rapport of person-to-person exchanges. The whole person communicates.
4. Cooperation and communication in an organization go hand in hand. When there is a mutual respect between people, spelling out rules and procedures for communicating is unnecessary.
5. There are several barriers to effective communications. These include failure to listen with respect and understanding, lack of skill in feedback, and misinterpreting the meanings of words used by the speaker. It is also common

practice to listen to what we want to hear, and tune out things we do not want to hear.
6. Communication is management's chief problem. The supervisor should accept the challenge to communicate more effectively and to improve interagency and intra-agency communications.
7. The supervisor may often plan for and conduct meetings. The planning phase is critical and may determine the success or the failure of a meeting.
8. Speaking before groups usually requires extra effort. Stage fright may never disappear completely, but it can be controlled.

J. Self-Development
1. Every employee is responsible for his own self-development.
2. Toastmaster and toastmistress clubs offer opportunities to improve skills in oral communications.
3. Planning for one's own self-development is of vital importance. Supervisors know their own strengths and limitations better than anyone else.
4. Many opportunities are open to aid the supervisor in his developmental efforts, including job assignments; training opportunities, both governmental and non-governmental—to include universities and professional conferences and seminars.
5. Programmed instruction offers a means of studying at one's own rate.
6. Where difficulties may arise from a supervisor's being away from his work for training, he may participate in televised home study or correspondence courses to meet his self-development needs.

K. Teaching and Training
1. The Teaching Process
Teaching is encouraging and guiding the learning activities of students toward established goals. In most cases this process consists of five steps: preparation, presentation, summarization, evaluation, and application.

   a. Preparation
   Preparation is two-fold in nature; that of the supervisor and the employee. Preparation by the supervisor is absolutely essential to success. He must know what, when, where, how, and whom he will teach. Some of the factors that should be considered are:
   1) The objectives
   2) The materials needed
   3) The methods to be used
   4) Employee participation
   5) Employee interest
   6) Training aids
   7) Evaluation
   8) Summarization

   Employee preparation consists in preparing the employee to receive the material. Probably the most important single factor in the preparation of the employee is arousing and maintaining his interest. He must know the objectives of the training, why he is there, how the material can be used, and its importance to him.

b. Presentation
In presentation, have a carefully designed plan and follow it. The plan should be accurate and complete, yet flexible enough to meet situations as they arise. The method of presentation will be determined by the particular situation and objectives.

c. Summary
A summary should be made at the end of every training unit and program. In addition, there may be internal summaries depending on the nature of the material being taught. The important thing is that the trainee must always be able to understand how each part of the new material relates to the whole.

d. Application
The supervisor must arrange work so the employee will be given a chance to apply new knowledge or skills while the material is still clear in his mind and interest is high. The trainee does not really know whether he has learned the material until he has been given a chance to apply it. If the material is not applied, it loses most of its value.

e. Evaluation
The purpose of all training is to promote learning. To determine whether the training has been a success or failure, the supervisor must evaluate this learning.
In the broadest sense, evaluation includes all the devices, methods, skills, and techniques used by the supervisor to keep himself and the employees informed as to their progress toward the objectives they are pursuing. The extent to which the employee has mastered the knowledge, skills, and abilities, or changed his attitudes, as determined by the program objectives, is the extent to which instruction has succeeded or failed.
Evaluation should not be confined to the end of the lesson, day, or program but should be used continuously. We shall note later the way this relates to the rest of the teaching process.

2. Teaching Methods
A teaching method is a pattern of identifiable student and instructor activity used in presenting training material.
All supervisors are faced with the problem of deciding which method should be used at a given time.

a. Lecture
The lecture is direct oral presentation of material by the supervisor. The present trend is to place less emphasis on the trainer's activity and more on that of the trainee.

b. Discussion
Teaching by discussion or conference involves using questions and other techniques to arouse interest and focus attention upon certain areas, and by doing so creating a learning situation. This can be one of the most

valuable methods because it gives the employees an opportunity to express their ideas and pool their knowledge.

c. Demonstration
The demonstration is used to teach how something works or how to do something. It can be used to show a principle or what the results of a series of actions will be. A well-staged demonstration is particularly effective because it shows proper methods of performance in a realistic manner.

d. Performance
Performance is one of the most fundamental of all learning techniques or teaching methods. The trainee may be able to tell how a specific operation should be performed but he cannot be sure he knows how to perform the operation until he has done so.
As with all methods, there are certain advantages and disadvantages to each method.

e. Which Method to Use
Moreover, there are other methods and techniques of teaching. It is difficult to use any method without other methods entering into it. In any learning situation, a combination of methods is usually more effective than any one method alone.

Finally, evaluation must be integrated into the other aspects of the teaching-learning process.

It must be used in the motivation of the trainees; it must be used to assist in developing understanding during the training; and it must be related to employee application of the results of training.

This is distinctly the role of the supervisor.

Kitchen Layouts
RECOMMENDATIONS FOR THE LAYOUT OF RESTAURANT KITCHENS

1. The floor area of a kitchen should include:

    A. The area occupied by the equipment.
    B. The spaces between equipment and the walls, and the spaces between equipment exclusive of aisle space.
    C. Aisle space.

2. Spacing of equipment:

    A. Aisle space should be a dequate for the operation and not less than 30" wide.
    B. All stoves, ovens, fryers, refrigerators, kitchen and food preparation and food service equipment should be spaced sufficiently from the wall so as to allow access for cleaning and inspection of all equipment. Inaccessible spaces which would become potential insect and rodent harborages should not be permitted. Distances of 12"-24" from the wall are recommended. If such space is not available, then the equipment should be sealed to the wall and floor.
    C. Stationary, tied-in units such as fountain, counter, and back bar units should be sealed to each other, thus eliminating crevices and open spaces.
    D. Dish and glass-washing machines should be spaced away from the wall to permit complete access for cleaning and repair.

3. Walls and ceilings in the kitchen and other food preparation rooms shall be constructed of a hard material and shall have a smooth finish. When the use of the premises results in the presence of steam or vapor, such as in dishwashing rooms or rooms containing steam kettles, and when required by the Department, the walls and ceilings shall be constructed of smooth cement, glazed tile, glazed brick, or other non-absorbent material. Walls and ceilings should be kept clean and in good repair.

4. The use of a metal covering on a wall or ceiling should be discouraged and permitted only where it can be installed in such a manner that all joints can be welded or soldered tight and smooth. Futhermore, the metal should be of sufficient gauge to prevent buckling and should be non-corrosive.

5. The use of wooden walls in kitchens and food preparation rooms is not desirable. The wall should be free of any pits, cracks, crevices, or protruding ledges. Baseboards or molding should be flush with the wall.

6. No paper or oilcloth coverings should be used on walls or restaurant kitchens of food preparation rooms.

7. The need for a tile-finished wall or an enamel paint-finished wall should be judged on the basis of the accessibility of the wall for cleaning purposes. If the equipment is placed in such proximity to the wall as to make it impossible to hand-brush or mop, then a tile wall is preferred so that it may be hosed down. If, on the other hand, there is adequate aisle space for a worker to clean the wall by hand, then an enamel-painted wall would be adequate, since repairs or repainting could be easily accomplished if necessary.

8. All defects in the walls behind the fixtures should be repaired and holes filled before the installation of fixtures, so as to prevent possible rodent and insect harborage.

9. Kitchen floors should be constructed of water-tight, non-absorbent material, impervious to moisture or grease. These materials may include:

    A. Trowel-finished smooth cement
    B. Terrazzo stone
    C. Packing house brick tile
    D. Asbestos vinyl tile
    E. Hardwood water-tight floor
    F. Any other suitable material that is impervious and water-tight.
    When it is deemed necessary by the Department, because the type of operation will result in wet floors or require frequent flushing of walls and floors, then the construction should be limited to items a, b, and c, and such floor should be graded and drained to a properly trapped sewer-connected sanitary drain. The juncture of the wall and floor should be coved to a flush finish. The use of linoleum or similar floor coverings is not recommended in kitchens and food preparation rooms.

10. Adequate ventilation should be provided for the kitchen, dishwashing room, toilet, locker rooms, food preparation areas, storerooms, cellar areas, and particularly in all sections having gas-burning units.

11. All hoods and ducts which carry off to the outer air any steam, gases, odors, or smoke, or any apparatus used for air-conditioning shall be constructed, operated, and maintained in such a manner so as not to be objectionable, or create a nuisance.

12. Suitable means should be provided for the protection of food against condensation from suspended pipes and possible leaks from overhead waste or sewer pipes.

13. The walls of the cellar may be whitewashed, provided that such cellar is not used for food preparation purposes.

14. The garbage room walls and floor should be constructed of concrete, cement, or other watertight, non-absorbent materials, so graded and drained as to discharge all liquid matter into a properly trapped floor drain. The garbage room should be adequately ventilated and water-supplied, and provided with water connections for cleansing the garbage cans. Refrigeration of the garbage room is desirable.

15. The entire kitchen premises shall be lighted adequately by natural or artificial means so as to permit the activity for which the premises are used to be carried on safely and to permit effective inspection and cleaning of the premises. It is recommended that a minimum of 20 foot-candles of light be maintained in the general kitchen area, while a minimum of 40 foot-candles be maintained in the areas requiring accurate observation.

16. One or more grease traps adequate in size to handle the total flow of waste water from the water-supplied kitchen fixtures should be installed in the kitchen waste line in accordance with approved plumbing code requirements.

17. All shelving should be spaced at least 2" from the wall and so constructed as to be readily accessible for cleaning. Bottom shelves should be at least 6" to 10" off the floor and the underpart open for cleaning. Wooden shelves in kitchens or stockrooms should not be painted. All shelves must be kept free of any oilcloth, paper, or other covering.

18. All cutting boards and work boards should be constructed so as to be readily removable for cleaning.

19. A dipper-well with an "over-the-rim" inlet with fresh running water should be provided for the storage of ice cream scoops at each ice cream dispensing station.

20. Provisions shall be made for the sanitary handling of ice intended for human consumption. The use of some device for handling the ice is required. The handle end of such device or any part of the human hand must not be permitted to come in contact with the ice. It is suggested that the scoop or other ice-handling device be hung up after each use.

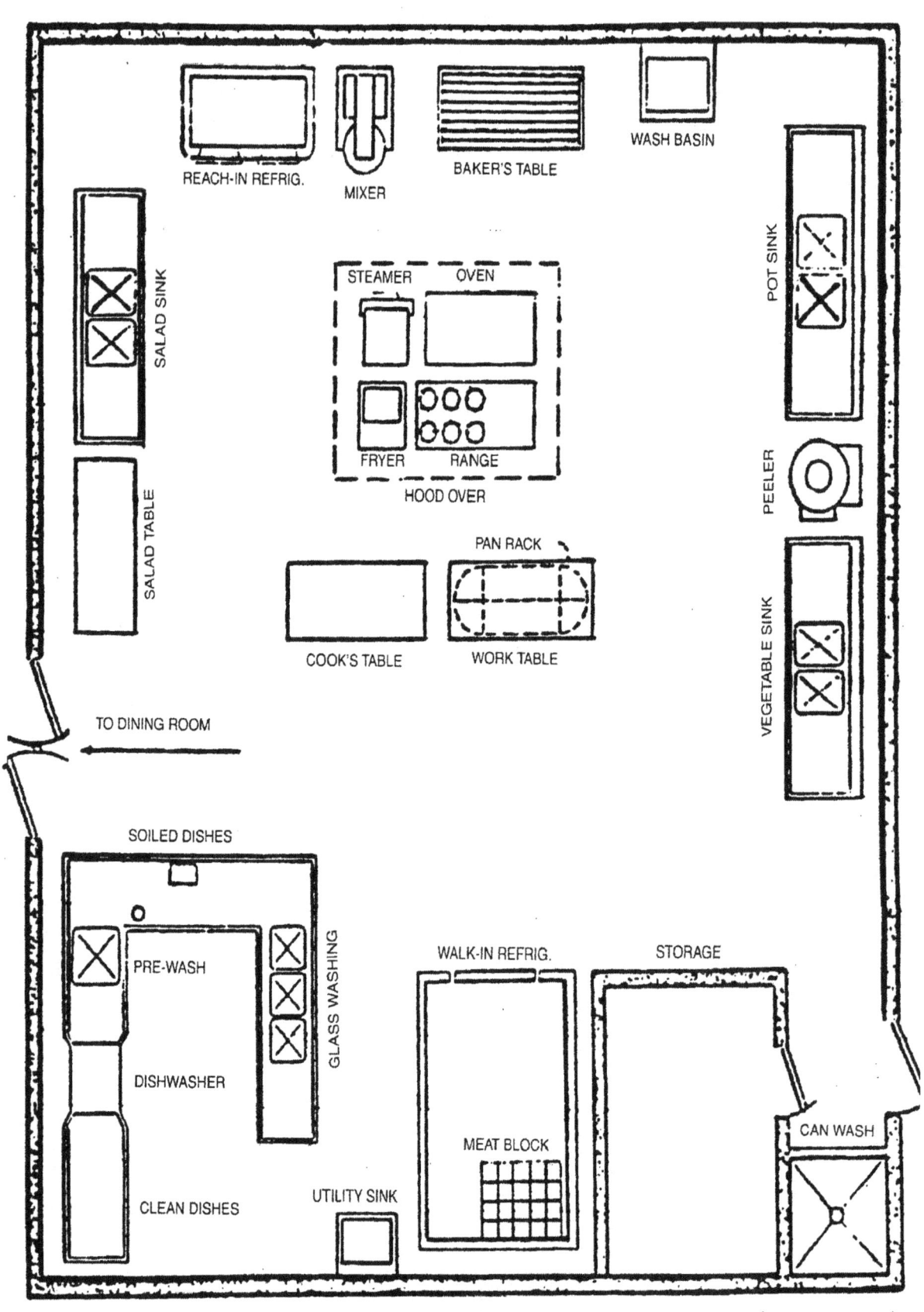

LAYOUT OF KITCHEN EQUIPMENT

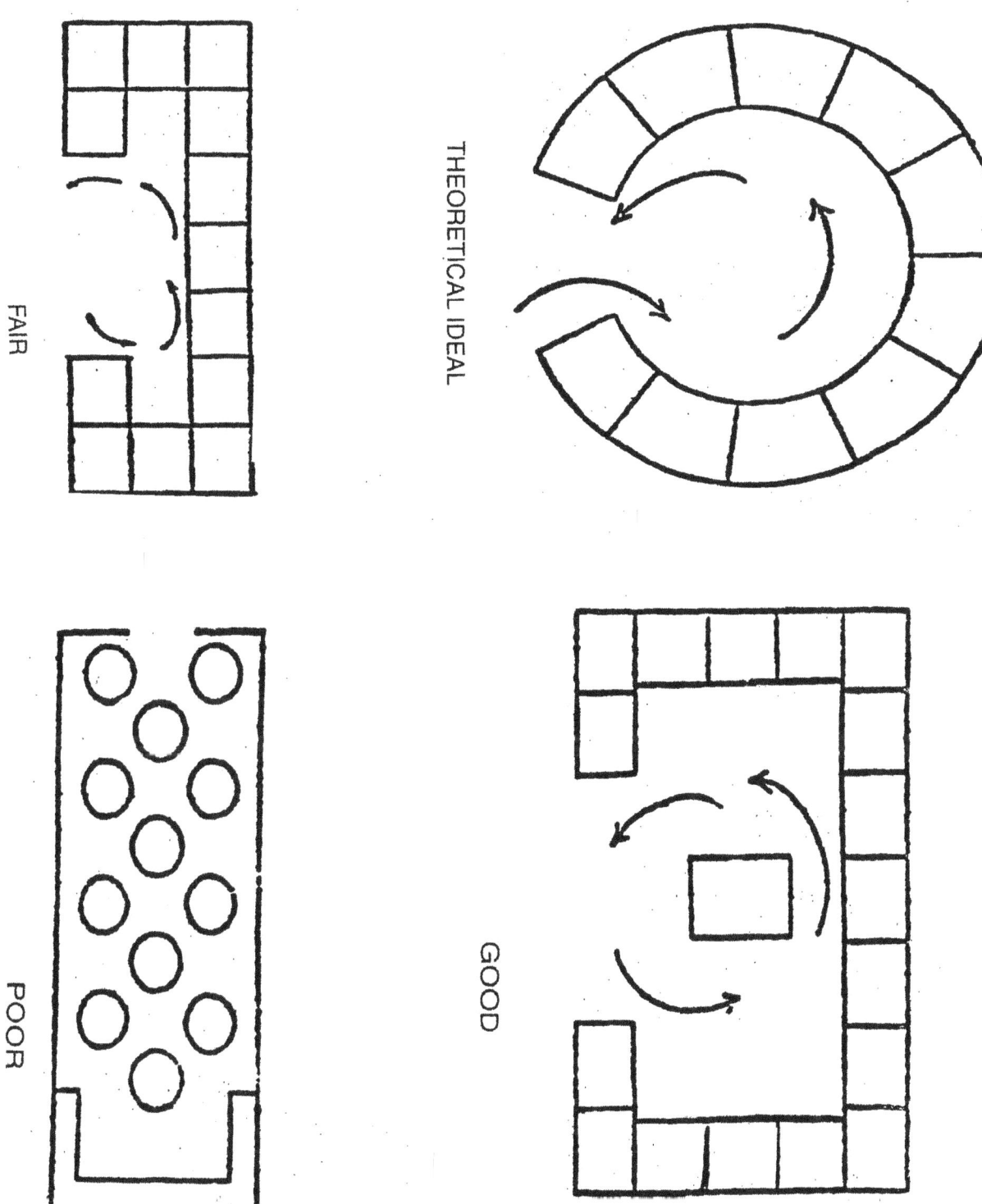

KITCHEN SAFETY
ACCIDENTS DON'T HAPPEN! THEY ARE CAUSED!

I. WHAT ARE THE COMMON ACCIDENTS?

1. Slips and Falls
2. Cuts
3. Burns
4. Bumps and Bruises
5. Electrical Shock
6. Overlifting

II. WHAT ARE THE CAUSES?

1. Inadequate Safety Instructions
2. Inadequate Maintenance
3. Carelessness
4. Haste
5. Employee Resistance to Training
6. Inadequate Equipment
7. Short Cuts
8. Improper Shoes

SAFETY
RULES AND
REGULATIONS

III. HOW CAN THEY BE PREVENTED

1. Good Management Attitude
2. Proper Employee Training
3. Good Equipment
4. Proper Construction
5. Excellent Housekeeping
6. Correct Traffic Patterns

GOOD
MAINTENANCE

HAVE FIRST AID FACILITIES AVAILABLE AND BE PREPARED TO PROVIDE AID!!

Food Sanitation Guide

INTRODUCTION

Restaurants, hotel and catering services in the country and the city serve millions of meals daily. This places tremendous responsibility upon them in safeguarding public health by preparing and serving only wholesome foods.

There are a number of cardinal principles which must be observed in preparing and serving wholesome foods. The bacterial contamination of these foods can be kept at a minimum if these principles are followed.

The food-handler must always be aware that he may contaminate the product by poor personal hygiene and work habits. He must always keep his person clean and work tools in a clean and sanitary condition.

Food must be stored in such a manner as to protect it from contamination. Unfortunately unless the food is sterilized, which is rarely practical, the presence of some bacteria is unavoidable. In order to keep their growth to a minimum, proper time and temperature control methods must be practiced.

Special care must be taken in the handling of foods which are to be served without further heat treatment. Ready-to-eat foods must not be subjected to contamination by coming into contact with unprocessed or partially processed foodstuffs or unsanitized work surfaces and implements.

Wholesome foods cannot be prepared in a dirty plant. The importance of good housekeeping cannot be minimized as a factor in the production of wholesome foods.

These general principles are more fully developed in the guide that follows.

I. Food Storage

The recommendations and prohibitions made below, if followed, will result in a wholesome and bacterialogically sound food product.

    A. Dry Storage Foods
1. Dry stored foods are to be protected against contamination by insects, rodents, dust and other types of dirt.
2. All food storage containers should be properly labeled.

    B. Cold Storage
1. Frozen foods
   (a) During storage frozen foods are to be completely frozen until ready for use. ($0°$ F)
   (b) The freezer should be equipped with a thermometer so freezer temperatures can be determined without entering the holding box.
   (c) Foods are to be stored in an orderly manner to assure cold air circulation and are not to be stored directly on the floor.

    C. Chilled Foods
1. Chilled foods should be kept at $45°F$ or less at all times. This may be done by the use of a walk-in refrigerator, reach-in refrigerator, refrigerated show cases, refrigerator counter and refrigerated tables, etc.
2. Refrigerators should be supplied with appropriate thermometers.
3. Containers holding foods should not be stored so that the bottom surface of the container rests on the surface of the food product in the container below it.
4. Cooked foods should be stored so that they do not become contaminated by raw foods.
5. All foodstuffs should be stored in such a manner as to protect them from contamination.

    D. Storage of Hot Foods

Foods to be served hot soon after cooking should not at any time be allowed to drop below an internal temperature of $14°$ F. If food is not to be served immediately upon completion of the cooking, it may be kept at temperatures in excess of $14°$ F by the use of warming cabinets, steamtables, chafing dishes or any other devices suitable for these purposes. Hot perishable foods are not to be kept at room temperature when the internal and surface temperature of the food falls below $140°$ F. Rare roast beef can be an exception to this. (See handling of rare roast beef, Pages 7-9)

II. Cleaning and Sanitization of Equipment and Kitchen Utensils

Equipment, utensils and work surfaces which come in contact with food should be thoroughly cleaned and sanitized before and after food preparation.

    A. Methods of Cleaning and Sanitizing

Prior to washing, manually remove all adhering food particles. Then wash, using a suitable soap or detergent, and hot water liberally applied by manual or mechanical means. After rinsing and removing all visible dirt and grease, sanitize using one of the following methods:

1. Heat Sanitization

   (a) Clean hot water, $170°$ F or more, applied to all surfaces of the equipment or utensils for at least 30 seconds.

2. Chemical Sanitization
(a) Apply a commercial preparation (Sodium Hypochlorite type) being sure to follow label directions.
(b) If a commercial product is not available or desired, a suitable solution may be prepared by mixing 1/2 ounce of household bleach, (5.25% Sodium Hypochlorite) in one gallon of lukewarm water (do not use hot water). Flood the surfaces of the equipment and utensils with this solution for at least one minute. Do not rinse or wipe after this operation.
If necessary to dry, air dry. Do not use a solution which is more than two hours old. If more solution is required, prepare a fresh supply.

III. Principles of Food Preparation and Services

During food preparation, improper techniques may contaminate the product with disease-causing organisms. It is for this purpose that sanitary procedures must be observed. Listed below are some principles which should be followed.

A. Food that is to be served cold should be kept cold ($45°$ F or less) through all stages of storage, processing, and serving. Thawing of frozen foods should be accomplished in such a manner so as to keep the surface and internal temperatures of the product $45°$ F or less at all times. If frozen food is to be thawed in water, running cold water is to be used.

B. Foods to be served hot are to be kept so that the internal and surface temperatures do not fall below $140°$ F. (See handling of rare roast beef - Pages 7-9). Care must be taken in the cooling of hot foods so they do not become contaminated by dust, contact with work clothes, human contact, etc. Cooling should be accomplished as quickly as possible by the use of fans, refrigeration, etc. To determine the temperature of foods, a food thermometer is to be used. (Hands are not to be used).

C. Partially processed and leftover foods are to be refrigerated at $45°$ F. or below. Just prior to service they are to be removed from the refrigerator and heated rapidly to serving temperatures so that the internal temperatures are not less than $140°$ F.

D. The holding of perishable foods between the temperatures of $140°$ and $45°$ F is to be kept at a minimum.

E. Contact of ready-to-eat foods with bare hands should be kept at an irreducible minimum and utensils should be used whenever possible.

F. Ready-to-eat foods should not be contaminated by coming in contact with work surfaces, equipment, utensils or hands previously in contact with raw foods until such surfaces, etc. have been cleaned and sanitized.

G. Do not place packing cases and cans on food work surfaces.

H. When necessary to taste foods during processing, a clean sanitized utensil should be used. When tasting again, either re-clean and re-sanitize utensil, or use another sanitized utensil.

I. Foods are to be cooked and processed as close to the time of service as possible.

J. Menu planning should be such as to prevent excessive leftovers, and leftovers are not to be pooled with fresh foods during storage.

IV. Transportation of Foods

In some food operations, it is necessary to transport food from a central kitchen (commissary) to an establishment where it is finally served. The food transported can be in a ready-to-eat state or a pre-cooked stage, which is finally processed at the place of service. The following practices should be observed to see that contamination is not introduced or possible previous bacterial contamination not afforded means for extensive multiplication during this period.

1. Transporting containers and vehicles should be clean and of sanitary design to facilitate cleaning.
2. Transporting containers and vehicles should have acceptable refrigerating and/or heating facilities for maintaining food at cold (45° F or below) or hot (above 140°) temperatures while in transit.
3. Food stored in transporting containers and vehicles should be protected from contamination.
4. A minimum amount of time is to be taken for the loading and unloading of foods from transporting vehicles so foods will not be exposed to adverse temperatures and conditions.

V. Food Processing Techniques Relative to Specific Types of Service
  A. Displayed Food (Buffet, Smorgasbord, etc.)
   1. Hot foods are to be kept at or above 140° F on the display table by use of chafing dishes, steam tables or other suitable methods.
   2. Cold foods are to be at temperatures 45° F. or less before being displayed and not to be exposed at room temperature for more than one hour unless some means is employed, (ice, mechanical refrigeration, etc.) to keep cold foods at or less than 45° F.
   3. All foods displayed and, therefore, subject to contamination must be discarded at the conclusion of the buffet service.
  B. Protein Type Salads (Tuna, Ham, Shrimp, Egg, Chicken, Lobster, etc.)

  These salads are always served cold and, therefore, all salad ingredients except the seasoning and spices are to be chilled to 45° F or less before use. Celery, which is almost always a component of these salads, should be treated so as to minimize its bacterial content by the immersing of the chopped celery in boiling water, using a hand strainer or colander for 30 seconds and then chilling immediately by holding under running cold tap water.

  Before the mixing operation, the previously washed can opener, and tops of cans and jars holding salad ingredients should be wiped with a clean cloth containing sanitizing solution. The salad ingredients should be mixed with clean, sanitizing equipment, (sanitary type masher, sanitary mixing bowl, stainless steel long handled spon or fork, mechanical tumbler type mixer, etc.). There should be an absolute minimum of bare hand contact with the equipment and ingredients. The mixing operation is to be completed as quickly as possible and the finished salad immediately served or refrigerated.
  C. Additional Instructions Relative to Specific Salads

1. Shrimp and Lobster Salad
   Immerse shrimp, or lobster meat in boiling water for 30 seconds and then chill to 45° F or less before adding to salad. Fast chilling can be accomplished by placing the meat in shallow pans in the freezer or refrigerator or on top of cracked ice.
2. Egg Salad
   After removing shell, use a hand strainer or colander to immerse hard-boiled eggs in boiling water for 30 seconds and then chill to 45° F or less before adding to salad. Chill the eggs by refrigerating or by placing strainer containing them under running cold tap water.
3. Chicken and/or Turkey Salad
   After removal from bones, immerse chicken or turkey meat in boiling water or boiling stock for 30 seconds and then chill to 45° F. before adding to salad. Fast chilling can be accomplished by placing the meat in shallow pans in the freezer, refrigerator or on cracked ice.
4. Ham Salad
   Immerse diced ham in boiling water or boiling stock for 30 seconds and then chill to 45° F. or less before adding to salad. Fast chilling can be accomplished by the same method used for chicken and shrimp.

D. Hot Meats and Poultry Served from Steamtables or Other Suitable Warming Devices
   1. Schedule the cooking of meats so they will be completed as close as possible to desired time of service.
   2. Upon removal from the oven or stove, cooked meats are to be kept at an internal temperature of 140° F or higher in a steamtable or other suitable device.
   3. Maintain the water in the steamtable at a temperature in excess of 180° F. The water must be brought to this temperature before any foods are placed therein. Water in the steamtable shall be kept at a steamtable depth so as to be in contact with the bottom and upper portions of the sides of the food container.
   4. Refrigerated ready-to-eat cooked meats, especially leftovers, gravies and stocks, are to be heated rapidly to an internal temperatures of 165° F or higher before being placed in the steamtable or warming device. Hot stock or meat gravies may be used to reheat meats. Steamtables or other warming devices should never be used to heat up cold meats.
   5. Cautions noted previously relative to hand contact, care of equipment storage, and menu planning should also be followed.

E. Roast Beef
   Because of consumer preference, roast beef is often served at an internal temperature of less than 140° F. Continuous warming and heating of this product, as for example on a steamtable, may not be practical as it causes the meat to become well done and thus less desirable to some consumers. It is, therefore, realized that instructions relative to maintenance of interior temperatures of meat cannot always be applied to this

product. It is essential, therefore, that Roast Beef be cooked as close to time of service as possible. Great care must be taken to prevent contamination. At large banquets this roast is sometimes stored or "rested" for excessive lengths of time, during which bacterial growth can occur.

1. Bone in Standing Rib Roast

    There are a number of methods to be used in the processing of this type of roast beef, which will help minimize bacterial contamination and growth.

    (a) Method No. 1

    The roast is boned and trimmed prior to cooking. Slicing is accomplished after cooking and immediately prior to serving. After removal from the oven, the surface temperature should be in excess of 140° F. This method minimizes the amount of handling after the cooking operations.

    (b) Method No. 2

    After cooking and storage the roast is boned, trimmed (all surfaces) and sliced immediately prior to service. This method removes almost all surface contamination.

    (c) Method No. 3

    The surface of the raw roast beef is coated with a concentration of coarse salt. The beef is cooked and stored with this coating intact and it is not removed until just prior to service, at which time, boning and trimming and slicing takes place. The salinity on the surface of the meat inhibits the bacterial growth. It has been found that after removal of the salt coating platibility of the meat is not impaired as there is practically no penetration of the salt into the edible portion of the meat.

2. Boneless Tied Roast Beef

    This type of roast beef is commonly machine sliced and used on sandwiches and platters. As stated above this type of roast beef is often desired rate where high internal temperatures cannot be applied.

    Menu planning should be such that the roast beef should be removed from the oven as close to the service time as possible.

    After removing a large roast beef from the oven, it should be cut into smaller pieces, each not to exceed 6 pounds. The surface temperature of the meat should not fall below 140°., at which time the roast can be sliced for immediate service and placed in the refrigerator, warming oven or steamtable. The refrigerator temperature should be below 45° F and steamtable temperature in excess of 140° F.

    It is suggested that only one piece of roast be kept for immediate service and the other pieces be stored in the refrigerator or warming device. At the end of the day any piece of roast beef which has been partially used should be considered as a leftover. This piece of meat must be refrigerated overnight, and before being reused it is to be heated to an internal temperature in excess of 165° F. It is realized that after cooking at these temperatures, this product cannot be served again as rare roast beef.

The slicing machine used for this product should be dissassembled and cleaned at the end of the day's work, and left disassembled. Before beginning slicing operations the next day, it is to be sanitized and reassembled.

3. Steamship (Steamer) Beef Roasts

This type of roast consists of the whole beef round (top and bottom) usually served rare and stored at inadequate temperatures (less that 140°). This product is almost always hand carved. (The term hand carved is used to denote that it is not machine sliced). There is no need for hand contact inasmuch as this meat is sliced with the use of a chef's knife and fork and transferred to the sandwich or platter using these utensils. Since the normal means to prevent contamination cannot be excercised, it is mandatory that only properly sanitized equipment be used and the food-handler exert particular care not to contaminate the product. As stated above in paragraph 2, any unused portion of this roast should be refrigerated, and before being served again cooked to an internal temperature of 165° F. It is again realized that after recooking at this temperature this product cannot be served as rare roast beef.

F. Rare Steaks

If these are not cooked immediately prior to service, it is sometimes the practice to singe the outer surface of the meat, and then store it at room temperature until the time of service. It is cooked by broiling and served immediately.

For this type of meat service, it is important that the storage period is not over one hour, the meat does not come in contact with contaminated work surfaces or hands and the meat is subjected to sufficient surface terminal heat treatment just before serving.

G. Pre-cooked Hamburger Patties

It has become a practice in some restaurants to pre-cook hamburger patties, and store them in a warmer or above the stove or grill until needed for service. In most cases the temperatures and lengths of time the meat is kept can be such as to allow the growth of pathogenic organisms.

If this type of food preparation is practiced, extreme care should be taken to see that this product is not stored for more than one hour, the food is not contaminated by unclean hands or work surfaces, and it receives a thorough heat treatment (exceeding 16° F) just prior to its consumption.

H. Pre-cooked Chicken - (Barbecued Style)

This product, a whole eviscerated chicken of 2-3 pounds, is usually cooked in a rotisserie-type radiant heating device and stored for varying lengths of time and temperature. Again this type of food storage is advantageous for the growth of food poisoning organisms.

Precautions to be followed with this product are: all parts of the poultry are to be thoroughly and completely cooked (over 165° F); it is to be handled and stored so that it will not come in contact with contaminated hands or work surfaces; and it shall not be kept at temperatures between 45° F and 14° F for more than one hour anytime prior to consumption.

I. Poultry Stuffing

Often times adequate internal temperatures are not obtained in the cooking of stuffed poultry. The temperature of the stuffing is such as to incubate rather than destroy bacteria. It is therefore advisable to cook the stuffing separately from the poultry. When this is done adequate temperatures (165° F) are reached in both the stuffing and poultry. Thereafter the stuffing should be handled and/ or stored in a manner similar to that noted previously for perishable protein foods.

J. Custard-Filled Baked Goods

The problems with custard fillings arise after completion of the cooking operation during the cooling and handling period. The following recommendations are made:

1. Utensils and receptacles must be sanitized as previously noted.
2. The finished custard should be transferred to shallow stainless steel or aluminum trays to facilitate rapid cooling. It is important at this point not to contaminate the product with the foodhandler's hands or clothing.
3. A long-bladed flexible spatula of sanitary construction should be used to scrape the residue from the cooking receptacle.
4. The finished product should be refrigerated as quickly as possible and at no time should the product be exposed to room temperature for more than one hour.
5. The shallow pans of custard should be covered with wax or other clean paper while cooling and while being stored in the refrigerator.
6. Jelly-filling machines of sanitary design should be used. Multiple use pastry bags, after washing, are to be boiled or sanitized before use. A single service pastry bag can be fashioned out of wax or parchment paper. A desire method of filling eclair shells, cream puffs and similar type products is to cut the shell in half and apply the filling with a properly sanitized stainless steel spatula. This is the only method to be used in the production of napoleans.
7. Butter cream which is to be used as an ingredient of custard should be handled with the same precautions as actual custard.
8. The finished product, immediately after completion, must be kept under refrigeration (45° F or less) at all times until consumed. Commercial fillings, bavarian creams, etc., are often used instead of true custard. They are used, as per label directions, and are sometimes used with the addition of eggs, cream, butter cream, etc., depending on the recipe of the individual food processor. The same care, relative to the boiling and refrigeration of all ingredients, should be taken in the manufacture of these products as is observed with true custard.

K. Deviled Eggs

It has been the experience of the Food Processing Control Unit that this product is needlessly contaminated by poor handling techniques. The following is suggested to minimize contamination.

1. This product is to be prepared as close to service as possible.
2. After the shell is removed from the egg, the peeled egg is to be placed in a strainer or colander and then in boiling water for not less than 30 seconds and then immediately placed in running cold water and chilled to 45° F or less.
3. At this point, when it is unavoidable that the bare hands be used, it is mandatory that the food handler wash his hands thoroughly with a germicidal soap before proceeding with the process.
4. Whenever possible remove the yolk of the egg with a sanitized utensil, and when the yolk is mashed and mixed with seasonings, a sanitized utensi' is also to be used.
5. In extruding the mashed yolk, a single service pastry bag is recommended. If a multiple use bag is desired it is to be sanitized by heat or chemical treatment prior to use.
6. If the finished product is not used immediately, it is to be refrigerated at 45° F or less until served.

L. Fresh Pork Products

Though it has been previously mentioned that meats are to be cooked to proper internal temperatures, it is felt that an additional warning be given concerning fresh pork products. Government inspection of fresh pork is not a guarantee against trichina contamination of this product. The trichina are not readily detectable except by microscopic examination and then only if an infested area is examined. It is therefore mandatory that fresh pork products be cooked to an internal temperature of at least 150° F.

M. Chopped Liver

This perishable, popular product is ordinarily literally manhandled in processing. Inasmuch as most of the handling takes place after cooking and the product is served without further heat treatment extra precautions must be taken to minimize hand contact.

Equipment must be cleaned and sanitized before use. It is best to clean, sanitize, and assemble equipment immediately prior to use. Ingredients should not be touched with bare hands after cooking. Cooked liver is to be handled with sanitized equipment only. Hard boiled eggs, after shells are removed, are to be placed in a colander or strainer and immersed in boiling water for 30 seconds and then placed in running cold water and chilled to 45°F or less. The peeled eggs are then to be handled by implements only. After mixing, the finished chopped liver is to be placed in stainless steel serving containers or molds without use of bare hands. If hand molding is required for a decorative display this is to be done immediately prior to service.

VI. Plant Sanitation and Maintenance

The unclean and defective condition of the physical plant, walls, floors, ceilings, doors, windows, etc., can adversely affect the final product from a bacterial standpoint. Care should be taken to see that they are clean and maintained in such a manner as to facilitate proper plant sanitation. It is known that bacterial organisms will establish themselves on encrusted foods such as is found on walls, light switches, room and refrigerator door handles, and other surfaces touched by food-handlers. Improper wall, window and door maintenance, ineffective cleaning and poor garbage disposal methods can also lead to insect and rodent infestations. These well known vectors of disease organisms can introduce food poisoning bacteria to foodstuffs in the establishment. (When necessary acceptable insecticides and rodenticides can be used to prevent or exterminate an infestation of these pests. Care should be observed to see they do not come in contact with foodstuffs.)

Adequate amounts of hot and cold running water should be supplied at properly maintained fixtures, strategically placed in parts of the plant, i.e., toilets, food processing areas, utensil cleaning areas, etc. Such fixtures should also be supplied with detergents, bactericides, and single service hand towels.

Equipment should be of sanitary design and maintained in a sanitary condition, cleaned after use and sanitized before use. Open seams and worn or defective surfaces which allow food particles to accumulate and prevent proper cleaning should be repaired forthwith.

Self-inspection and cleaning schedules should be devised for all areas of the plant and equipment. At routine periods all areas should be inspected to detail and findings noted on a form devised for this purpose. Follow-up on findings should be made as soon as feasible.

Cleaning and maintenance should follow every major production period. If production is continuous for a 12 or 18 hour period, "down" periods should be incorporated in the work schedule to allow for this sanitation program.

VII. Non-Commercial Food Operations

This guide is primarily for the use of the sanitarian and the operators of commercial food-processing establishments. In a city of this size, many large meals and buffets are prepared and served by private and volunteer organizations. These include church and synogogue socials, local charity and fund raising affairs, fraternal organizations, etc.

These types of affairs often lead to food-borne illnesses when proper precautions are not taken. It is therefore important that the recommendations contained herein also be practiced by these large non-commercial feeding operations.

VIII. Assistance to Food Processors

Commercial and non-commercial food operations are urged to use the expertise of this department by calling upon us to discuss and analyze problems occuring in their food handling programs.

SALAD PREPARATION GUIDE

1. Refrigerate all salad ingredients except seasoning and spices overnight or chill to $45°$ F or lower before use.
2. Purchase a sanitizing solution or prepare one by mixing one or two ounces of bleach to a gallon of cold water. This solution is effective for approximately two hours. Prepare a fresh solution if further sanitization is needed.
3. Clean work surfaces, equipment and utensils (pots, pans, spoons, spatulas, etc.) with soap and hot water, rinse with clean water, and then give a final rinse with sanitizing solution. Stainless steel utensils and equipment are preferred in preparation of these foods.
4. Clean hands, fingernails, and arms thoroughly with ger-micidal soap and hot water and dry with single use paper towels.
5. Individuals preparing salads are not to perform other tasks while engaged in salad preparation.
6. Clean and sanitize tops of cans and jars before openings. Do not use fingers to pry off can lids or drain off liquid contents.
7. Place diced celery, including pre-cut packaged celery in a strainer and immerse in boiling water for 30 seconds; then chill to $45°$ F or less.
8. Use clean sanitized utensils in mixing and handling of foods. Avoid hand contact with foods.
9. Refrigerate final salad product immediately in shallow pans.
10. Salads placed in bain-marie cold plates should have a minimum internal temperature of $45°$ F.
11. Do not fill trays above spill line.

Food Preparation-Handling and Storage

1. FOOD PREPARATION

    Begin with clean, fresh food. Handle food only when necessary.

    Don't dip fingers into food or use a stirring spoon to taste.

    Use oysters, clams and other frozen foods, fluid milk products and frozen milk desserts from approved sources.

    Never lean or sit on work surfaces.

    Foods should never be prepared in yards, alleys, stairs or hallways.

    Keep food that is on display covered so it can't be touched or coughed on by customers or contaminated by flies and other bugs.

    Always follow the recipe. Cook custards and cream sauces well. Chill them at once.

    Wash thoroughly with brush and clean water all vegetables and fruits which are to be served raw.

    As a food safeguard, boil leftover vegetables, gravies, soups, and other liquid foods before serving.

    Make sure that all mixing, grinding and chopping machines are thoroughly cleaned after each use. In order to properly clean one of these machines, one should know how to take it apart and assemble it.

    Work only in a well-lighted area that is well-ventilated.

2. FOOD STORAGE AND HANDLING

    Food should be stored well off the floor, away from walls or dripping pipes.

    Keep all food, bulk or otherwise, covered and safe from contamination.

    Check food daily and throw away any spoiled or dirty food.

    Store cleaning, disinfection, insect and rodent-killing powders and liquids away from foods, PLAINLY MARKED.

    Keep foods in refrigerator at temperature of 45° F or below.

    Check the temperature regularly with a good thermometer.

    Keep all cooling compartments closed except when you're using them.

    Store food in a refrigerator in such a way that inside air can circulate freely.

    Always refrigerate meats, creamed foods and custard desserts.

    Keep all refrigerated foods covered, and use up stored leftovers quickly.

    When dishes and utensils are sparkling clean, keep them that way by proper storage. Keep all cups and glasses inverted.

    Cakes, doughnuts and fruit pies may be kept inside a covered display area.

    The only goods that should be left on the counter uncovered are those which are wrapped and do not contain anything which could spoil at room temperature.

    Don't set dirty dishes, pots, cartons or boxes on food tables.

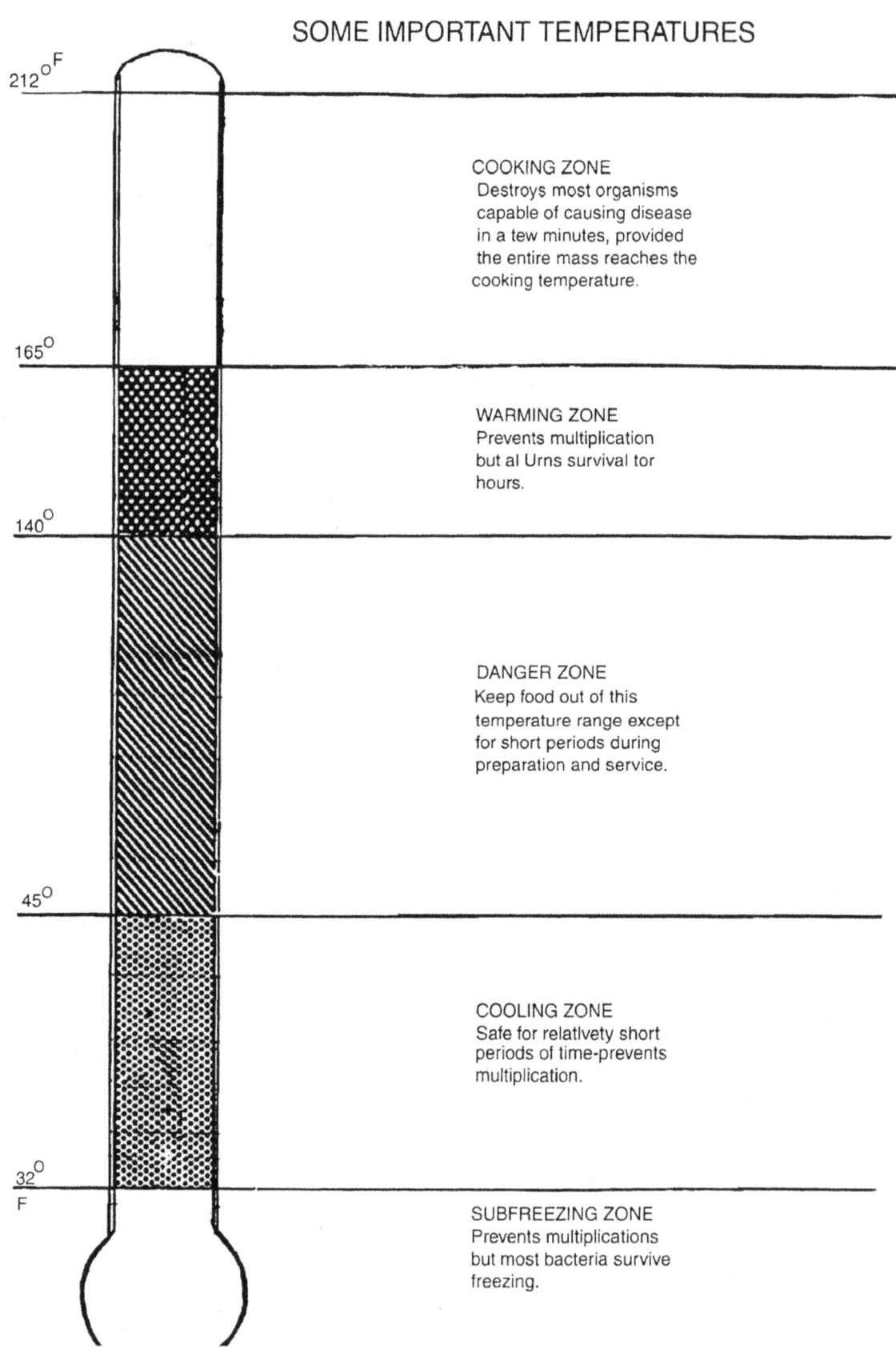

TEMPERATURE RANGE FOR SAFE STORAGE OF FOODS

Zone I Sub-freezing temperatures $0°$ F to $-15°$ F ($-18°$ to $-9.4°$ C)

- A. Frozen meat, fish, and vegetables
- B. Frozen fruits
- C. Ice Cream
- D. Homemade frozen deserts

Zone II High Humidity (85%) and Moderate Air Circulation $34°$ to $37°$ F ($1.1°$ to $2.7\ °C$)

- A. Fresh meat, chicken, and fish
- B. Sliced smoked ham and bacon
- C. Sliced cold cuts of meat
- D. Leftover canned and cooked meat

Zone III $38°$ to $40°$ F ($3.3°$ to $4.4°$ C)

- A. Fresh milk, cream, and buttermilk
- B. Cottage cheese and butter (both covered)
- C. Fresh orange and tomato juice (covered)
- D. Bottled beverage (for chilling)

Zone IV $40°$ to $43°$ F ($4.4°$ to $6.1°$ C) Moderate Humidity

- A. Berries, pears, and peaches
- B. Ripe grapefruit and oranges
- C. Ripe tomatoes (short time only)
- D. Fresh eggs
- E. Margarine
- F. Custards and puddings (day or two only)
- G. Prepared salads (for chilling)

Zone V $40°$ to $45°$ F ($4.4°$ to $7.2°$ C) High Humidity

- A. Cherries and cranberries
- B. Lettuce and celery
- C. Spinach, kale, and other greens
- D. Beets, carrots, parsnips, and turnips
- E. Peas and lima beans
- F. Cucumbers and eggplant (short time only)

Zone VI $55°$ to $60°$ F ($12.7°$ to $15.1°$ C) Fairly High Humidity and Moderate Circulation. (Good Fruit Cellar or Storage Cellar Well Ventilated).

- A. Apples, cabbage, potatoes, pumpkin, squash, unripened tomatoes, and maple syrup (in tight container)

Zone VII   Normal Room Temperature. Dry Storage
- A. Ready prepared cereals
- B. Crackers
- C. Bottled beverages

Zone VIII   Normal Room Temperature Storage

- A. Peanut Butter and honey
- B. Salad oils and vegetable shortenings
- C. Catsup and pickles
- D. Jelly and preserves
- E. Dried fruits and bananas (short time)
- F. Flour
- G. Dried peas and beans
- H. Sugar and salt

MICROBIOLOGY OF FOODS: BACTERIA

In order to understand the reasons behind food sanitation practices, it is necessary to know a few facts about the microorganisms which cause food spoilage and foodborne disease.

Bacteria, commonly called germs, are extremely small, plant-like organisms which must be viewed through a microscope in order to be seen. If 25,000,000 bacteria were placed in a line, that line would be only one inch long; one million could fit on the head of a pin. Like any living thing, bacteria require food, moisture, and the proper temperature for growth. Most of them need air, but some can thrive only in the absence of air (these are called anaerobic) and some can grow with or without air (facultative). Bacteria are found everywhere on the earth, in the air, and in the water. Soil abounds with bacteria which grow on dead organic matter.

SHAPES OF BACTERIA

One method of classifying bacteria is by their shape. All bacteria can be assigned to one of the following categories.

A. Cocci (plural of coccus) are round or spherical in shape. While they are able to live alone, they often exist in groups. Single chains are called streptococci. Those which form a grape-like cluster are called staphylococci, while those that form pairs are called diplococci. Some bacteria are named after the portion of the human anatomy they infect; for example, pneumococci infect the lungs, enterococci infect the intestines, and meningococci infect the meninges (protective sheath around the brain). Some of the common diseases caused by the cocci group are pneumonia, septic sore throat, scarlet fever, and meningitis.

B. Bacilli (plural of bacillus) are rod-shaped. Some of these also congregate in the single chain form, and are called streptobacilli. Some common diseases caused by bacilli are typhoid fever, tuberculosis, and anthrax.

C. Spirilla (plural of spirillum) are spiral or comma-shaped. Diseases caused by spirilla include cholera and syphilis.

SPORES

Some bacilli are able to protect themselves under adverse conditions by forming a protective shell or wall around themselves; in this form they are in the non-vegetative stage and are called spores. These bacterial spores can be likened to the seeds of a plant which are also resistant to adverse conditions. During the spore stage, bacteria do not reproduce or multiply. As soon as these spores find themselves under proper conditions of warmth, moisture, food and possibly air requirements. they resume their normal (vegetative) stage, and resume their growth. Since spores are designed to withstand rigorous conditions, they are difficult to destroy by the normal methods. Much higher killing temperatures and longer time periods are required. Fortunately, there are only a relatively few pathogenic or disease-causing bacilli which are spore formers. Tetanus, anthrax, and botulism are diseases caused by spore formers.

BACTERIAL REPRODUCTION

Bacteria reproduce by splitting in two, this is called binary fission. For this reason, their numbers are always doubling: one bacterium generates two; each of these generates two, resulting in a new total of four: etc. The time it takes for bacteria to double (generation time) is roughly fifteen to thirty minutes under good conditions.

TYPES OF BACTERIA ACCORDING TO THEIR EFFECT ON MAN

Types of bacteria, classified according to their effect on us, are:

      A. Harmful or disease-producing
      B. Undesirable
      C. Beneficial
      D. Benign

    A. Harmful or disease-producing bacteria are known as pathogenic bacteria or pathogens. They cause various diseases of man, animals, and plants.

    B. Undesirable bacteria, which cause decomposition of foods, are often referred to as putrefying bacteria. Bacteria that act on sugars in food, resulting in souring, are called saccharolytic bacteria.

    C. Beneficial bacteria are used in the production of various foods, including cultured milk, yogurt, cheese, and sauerkraut.

    The large intestine, or colon, contains millions of bacteria which are normal inhabitants of the intestinal tract, and we call this type *"coliform"* bacteria. It can be seen, therefore, that where coliform bacteria are found in food or water, they are an indication of fecal contamination. The coliforms themselves are not pathogenic, but where fecal contamination occurs, it is probable that other pathogenic organisms from the intestine may be present. The presence of coliform bacteria is often used as an index of good or bad sanitary practices.

    Bacteria are essential in the operation of certain sewage disposal plants, known as *"activated sludge plants"*. In these plants the bacteria digest the organic sewage and either liquefy the solid matter which is in colloid form, or change it so that it settles out.

    The greatest number of bacteria are found in the soil where they thrive on dead organic matter. They are constantly decomposing it, so that eventually it is changed into an inorganic form. This essential process of nature makes it possible for plants to absorb inorganic nutriment. Other types of bacteria *"fix"* nitrogen from the air, forming nitrates in the soil, generally on the roots of legumes.

    D. Benign bacteria, as far as we know at the present time, are neither helpful nor harmful to man. Of the hundreds of thousands of strains of bacteria, most fall into this category.

    It must be realized that may bacteria are essential in the balance of nature, and the destruction of all bacteria in the world would be catastrophic. Our main objective in public health protection, in which food handling plays a vital role, is the control and destruction of the pathogenic bacteria and those that cause food spoilage.

CONDITIONS FOR GROWTH

    A. Food - Bacterial require food for growth. Food must be absorbed in liquid form through the cell wall of the organism. Generally bacteria prefer neutral foods (ph 6-8) but some can thrive on highly acid or alkaline media.

    B. Moisture - Moisture (water) is an essential requirement. If moisture is not present, bacteria will not multiply and eventually may die. Processes which depend on removing available water, i.e., water in liquid form, from bacteria are used to preserve foods. Such methods include dehydration, freezing, and preserving in salt or sugar.

    C. Temperature - In general, bacteria prefer a warm temperature and grow best between 90-100° F. (Optimum temperature) The temperature of the body, 98.6° F, is excellent for bacterial growth; when bacteria are cultured in the laboratory, they are kept at this temperature. However, different types of bacteria prefer different temperatures, and are as follows:

    <u>Mesophilic</u>: Grow best at temperatures between 50-110° F. Most bacteria are in this group.

<u>Thermophilic</u>: Love heat. These grow best at temperatures between 110-150° F. or more

<u>Psychrophilic</u>: Love cold. These grow best at temperatures below 50° F.

Where heat is employed to destroy pathogenic bacteria, the food processor often must contend with thermophilic or thermoduric bacteria, which may withstand the pasteurizing or sterilizing processes. These bacteria are not pathogenic, but may be putrefactive.

D. Air - With respect to air atmospheric oxygen, we find that some bacteria can grow only where air is present; these are called aerobes. Some bacteria can grow only in a medium where air is absent, and these are called anaerobes. They can thrive in a sealed can, jar, or bottle of food. Those bacteria which prefer to live where air is present but may grow without air are termed facultative aerobes, and those which prefer to grow in the absence of air but may grow where air is present are called facultative anaerobes.

LOCOMOTION

Bacteria cannot crawl, fly, or move about. A few types do have thread-like appendages called flagella, with which they can propel themselves to a very limited extent. Therefore, they must be carried from place to place by some vehicle or through some channel. The channels of transmission include: air, water, food, hands, coughing, sneezing, insects, rodents, dirty equipment, unsafe plumbing connections, and unclean utensils. Hands are one of the most dangerous vehicles. There is no doubt that better care of food handlers' hands would aid greatly in cutting down the transmission of disease.

DESTRUCTION BY HEAT

The most reliable and time-tested method of destroying bacteria is heat. This method is effective only when both time and temperature factors are applied. In other words, not only do we have to reach the desired temperature to kill bacteria, but we must allow sufficient time to permit the heat to kill the more sturdy members. The lower the temperature (to certain limits, of course) the longer the time required to kill bacteria. Conversely, the higher the temperature, the less time is necessary. An example of this principle involves the two accepted methods for pasteurizing milk. In the *"holding"* method, milk is held at a temperature of 145° F for thirty minutes. In the more recently developed *"flash"* or *"high temperature-short time"* method, milk is held at 161° F for fifteen seconds.

In sterilizing foods for canning, the type of food and size of the containers must be taken into consideration in determining the proper time and temperature. The smaller the container, the faster the heat will be conducted through the food.

It is important to note once more that in order to destroy spore-forming bacilli completely, very high temperatures, often higher than 212° F are required for long time periods.

DESTRUCTION BY CHEMICALS

Bacteria can be destroyed by chemical agents. Those which kill all bacteria are called germicides or bactericides. Examples are phenol (carbolic acid), formaldehyde, iodine, chlorine, and others, such as the group of chemicals known as quarternary compounds. The effectiveness of the chemical bactericide depends on the concentration and the method with which it is used. If it is used to kill pathogenic organisms only, it is called a disinfectant. If a mild concentration is used on wounds to inhibit the growth of disease organisms, it is called an antiseptic. Some chemicals have been used in foods to inhibit the growth of spoilage bacteria, and these are called preservatives. Examples of these are sulphur dioxide, benzoate of soda, salt, sugar, and vinegar.

OTHER METHODS OF DESTRUCTION

When exposed to air and sunlight, bacteria are destroyed due to the combined effects of lack of moisture and food and exposure to the natural ultraviolet rays of the sun. Ultraviolet lamps are used for bactericidal purposes but their field is limited. Aeration is not used commercially as the sole means of sterilizing a product.

REFRIGERATION

Refrigeration of foods in refrigerators (32-45° F) does not kill bacteria. However, these temperatures do inhibit the growth of bacteria, both putrefactive and pathogenic, so that foods under proper refrigeration remain wholesome and free from disease for some time.

MICROBIOLOGY OF FOODS: BACTERIA AND OTHER MICROORGANISMS

Extremely low freezing temperatures for prolonged periods may result in the death of some bacteria, while others may survive. However, refrigeration or freezing should never be considered as a means of destroying bacteria; these methods merely retard bacterial growth.

VIRUSES

Viruses are minute organic forms which seem to be intermediate between living cells and organic compounds. They are smaller than bacteria, and are sometimes called filterable viruses because they are so small that they can pass through the tiny pores of a porcelain filter which retain bacteria. They cannot be seen through a microscope (magnification of 1500 x) but can be seen through an electron microscope (magnification of 1,000,000 x). Viruses cause poliomyelitis, smallpox, measles, mumps, encephalitis, influenza, and the common cold. Viruses, like bacteria are presumed to exist everywhere.

YEASTS

Yeasts are one-celled organisms which are larger than bacteria. They, too, are found everywhere, and require food, moisture, warmth, and air for proper growth. Unlike some bacteria which live without air, yeasts must have air in order to grow. They need sugar, but have the ability to change starch into sugar. When yeasts act on sugar, the formation of alcohol and carbon dioxide results. In the baking industry, yeast is used to *"raise dough"* through the production of carbon dioxide. The alcohol is driven off by the heat of the oven. In wine production, the carbon dioxide gas bubbles off, leaving the alcohol. The amount of alcohol produced by yeasts is limited to 18%, because yeasts are killed at this concentration of alcohol.

Yeasts reproduce by budding, which is similar to binary fission. Generally, the methods described for the destruction of bacteria will kill yeasts as well.

Yeasts are not generally considered to be pathogenic or harmful although a few of them do cause skin infections. Wild yeasts or those that get into a food by accident rather than by design of the food processor cause food spoilage and decomposition of starch and sugar, and therefore are undesirable.

MOLDS

Molds are multicellular (many-celled) microscopic plants which become visible to the naked eye when growing in sufficient quantity. Mold colonies have definite colors (white, black, green, etc.) They are larger than bacteria or yeasts. Some molds are pathogenic, causing such diseases as athletes' foot, ringworm, and other skin diseases. However, moldy foods usually do not cause illness. In fact, molds are encouraged to grow in certain cheeses to produce a characteristic flavor.

The structure of the mold consists of a root-like structure called the mycelium, a stem (ariel filament) called the hypha, and the spore sac, called the sporangium. All molds reproduce by means of spores. Molds are the lowest form of life that have these specialized reproductive cells.

Molds require moisture and air for growth and can grow on almost any organic matter, which does not necessarily have to be food. Molds do not require warmth, and grow very well in refrigerators. Neither do molds require much moisture, although the more moisture present, the better they multiply.

Methods of destruction for molds are similar to those required for bacteria. Heat, chemicals, and ultraviolet rays destroy mold spores as well as the molds. Refrigeration does not necessarily retard their growth.

Certain chemicals act as mold inhibitors. Calcium propionate (Mycoban) is one used in making bread. This chemical when used in the dough, retards the germination of mold spores, and bread so treated will remain mold-free for about five days.

One of the most beneficial molds is the Penicillium mold from which penicillin, an antibiotic, is extracted. The discovery, by Dr. Alexander Fleming, of the mold's antibiotic properties open up a whold field of research, and other antibiotic products from molds have been discovered.

CLASSIFICATION OF FOODBORNE DISEASE

Several terms are used to describe illness in which the causative agent is obtained by ingestion of food; the expression *"food poisoning"* is commonly employed to describe any of these. However, such usage is inaccurate and confusing.

Foodborne diseases caused by bacteria are divided into two classes. The first is called food intoxication (this is the real food poisoning) and designates illnesses due to toxins (poisons) secreted by bacteria growing in large numbers on the food prior to ingestion. In the second type of bacterial disease, called food infection, the symptoms are caused by the activity of large numbers of bacterial cells, having grown to some extent in the contaminated food, within the gastrointestinal system of the victim.

Other microbial contaminants of food, such as viruses, rickettsiae, and protozoa, can cause disease, as can other parasites. Chemical poisonings are characterized by a relatively sudden onset of symptoms, often in minutes. In addition, certain plants and animals contain chemical poisons, some of which produce illness within a short period after ingestion.

I. Food Intoxications
    A. Botulism
        1. Toxins are produced by growth of Clostridium botulinum in foods under anaerobic conditions. There are six major types of toxins: A, B, C, D, E and F. Types A, B, and E affect man. Antitoxins exist, although few hospitals routinely stock them.
        2. Symptoms: Toxin affects the central nervous system, producing difficulty in swallowing, double vision, and difficulty in speech and respiration, followed by death from paralysis of muscles of respiration.
        3. Onset of symtoms: 2 hours to 8 days, average 1 to 2 days.
        4. Inactivation of toxins: 15 minutes at $212°$ F.
        5. Foods usually involved: home-canned, low-acid vegetables. On rare occasions, commercially packed tuna, smoked fish, mushrooms, and vichysoisse.
    B. Staphylococcus Food Poisoning
        1. Toxin produced by coagulase positive Staphylococcus aureus.
        2. Symptoms: Nausea, vomiting, diarrhea, acute prostration, and abdominal cramps.
        3. Onset of symptoms: 1 to 6 hours, average 2-3 hours.
        4. Inactivation of toxin: Not inactivated by normal cooking times and temperatures.
        5. Foods usually involved: Ham, poultry, cream-filled bakery goods, protein salads.

II. Bacterial Food Infections
    A. Salmonellosis
        1. Salmonella typhimurium, Salmonella enteritidis, and others.
        2. Symptoms: Abdominal pain, diarrhea, chills, fever, frequent vomiting, and prostration.
        3. Onset of symptoms: 7 to 12 hours; average 12 to 24 hours.
        4. Inactivation: $165°$ F for period of cooking or heating.
        5. Foods usually involved: poultry, poultry products, inadequately cooked egg products, meats, and other foods.

- B. Bacillary dysentery (Shigellosis)
    1. Various species of Shigella (Shigella dysenteriae, Shigella sonnei, and others.)
    2. Symptoms: Diarrhea, bloody stools, fever.
    3. Onset of symptoms: 1 to 7 days; average 2-3 days.
    4. Inactivation: 165° for period of cooking.
    5. Foods usually involved: Moist prepared foods and dairy products contaminated with excreta from carrier.
- C. Streptococcal Infections (Scarlet fever or septic sore throat)
    1. Certain strains of beta-hemolytic streptococci
    2. Symptoms: Fever, sore throat.
    3. Onset of symptoms: 1 to 7 days; average 3 days.
    4. Inactivation: 165° F for period of cooking.
    5. Foods usually involved: Food contaminated with nasal or oral discharges from a case or carrier; raw milk from infected cows.
- D. Enterococci (Fecal Streptococci)
    1. Various strains of Streptococcus fecalis.
    2. Symptoms: Nausea, sometimes vomiting and diarrhea.
    3. Onset of symptoms: 2 to 18 hours
    4. Inactivation: 165° F for period of cooking.
    5. Foods usually involved: Prepared food products contaminated with excreta.
- E. Clostridium Perfringens
    1. Growth of Clostridium perfringens in food under anaerobic conditions.
    2. Symptoms: Acute abdominal pain and diarrhea, nausea, and rarely, vomiting.
    3. Onset of symptoms: 8 to 22 hours; average 8-12 hours.
    4. Inactivation: Variable, usually not inactivated by cooking temperatures.
    5. Foods usually involved: Poultry and meat products.

III. Viral Infections
- A. Infectious Hepatitis
    1. Virus of infectious hepatitis
    2. Symptoms: Fever, lack of appetite, malaise, fatigue, headache, nausea, chills, vomiting, jaundice may be present.
    3. Onset of symptoms: 14 to 35 days, average 25 days.
    4. Inactivation: not known.
    5. Foods usually involved: Shellfish (oyster, clams, mussels) taken from polluted waters and eaten raw; foods contaminated with excreta from an infected person.

IV. Parasitic Infections
- A. Trichinosis
    1. Trichinella spiralis.
    2. Symptoms: Nausea, vomiting, diarrhea (during digestion of trichinae); muscular pains, fever labored breathing, swelling of eyelids. Occassionally fatal.

3. Onset of symptoms: 2 to 28 days; average 9 days.
4. Inactivation: All parts of meat must reach 150° F to destroy cysts.
5. Foods usually involved: Raw or insufficiently cooked pork and pork products. Whale, seal, bear, and walrus meat have also been implicated.

B. Tapeworm (Taeniasis)
1. Taenia saginata (beef tapeworm); Taenia solium (pork tapeworm).
2. Symptoms: Beef tapeworm: abdominal pain, hungry feeling, vague discomfort. Pork tapeworm: varies from mild chronic digestive disorder to severe malaise.
3. Onset of symptoms: Several weeks.
4. Inactivation: All parts of the meat must reach 150° F.
5. Foods usually involved: Raw or insufficiently cooked beef or pork containing live larvae.

C. Fish Tapeworm Disease (Diphyllobothriasis)
1. Diphyllobothrium latum.
2. Symptoms: Anemia in heavy infections.
3. Onset of symptoms: 3 to 6 weeks.
4. Inactivation: All parts of fish meat must reach 150° F.
5. Foods usually involved: Raw or insufficiently cooked fish containing live larvae.

D. Amebic Dysentery
1. Entamoeba histolytica
2. Symptoms: Chronic diarrhea of varying severity or diarrhea alternating with constipation; occasionally fatal.
3. Onset of symptoms: 5 days to several months; average 3 to 4 weeks.
4. Inactivation: Cysts on vegetables destroyed by heating 30 minutes in water at 122° F.
5. Foods usually involved: Moist food contaminated with excreta from a carrier; contaminated water.

V. Poisonous Plants
A. Mushroom poisoning
1. Symptoms caused by phalloidine and other alkaloids of certain species of mushrooms.
2. Symptoms: Salivation: abdominal pain, intense thirst, nausea, vomiting, water stools, excessive perspiration, flow of tears; often fatal.
3. Onset of symptoms: 15 minutes to 15 hours.
4. Inactivation: Not inactivated by cooking.
5. Foods usually involved: Wild mushrooms, such as Amanita phalloides and Amanita muscaria, which are mistaken for edible mushrooms.

VI. Dangerous Chemicals
A. Antimony

1. Occurrence: Chipped grey enamelware in contact with acid foods and beverages.
2. Symptoms: Nausea, violent vomiting.
3. Onset of symptoms: 15 to 30 minutes.
4. Duration: Several hours.

B. Cadmium
   1. Occurence: Cadmium used as plating, e.g., ice cube trays, dissolved in food or beverages.
   2. Symptoms: Propulsive vomiting, nausea.
   3. Onset of symptoms: 15 to 30 minutes.
   4. Duration: Several hours.

C. Cyanide
   1. Occurrence: Foods contaminated with silver polish containing cyanide.
   2. Symptoms: Cyanosis (bluish discoloration of skin) mental confusion, glassy eyes, blue lips, often fatal.
   3. Onset of symptoms: Almost instantaneous.

D. Lead
   1. Occurrence: Food containers, solder containing more that 5% lead used on food equipment.
   2. Symptoms: Blue line on gums, cramps in stomach, bowels, and legs, constipation, loss of appetite, headache, irritability.

E. Copper
   1. Occurrence: Foods contaminated by copper salts (verdigris) on unclean copper utensils; beverages containing copper salts due to action of carbonation (carbon dioxide and water) on copper tubing.
   2. Symptoms: Vomiting, abdominal pain, diarrhea.
   3. Onset of symptoms: Usually immediate.

F. Zinc
   1. Occurrence (rare): Acid foods cooked in galvanized (zinc-plated) utensils.
   2. Symptoms: Dizziness, nausea, vomiting, tightness of throat.
   3. Onset of symptoms: a few minutes to two hours.

G. Nitrites
   1. Occurrence: Contamination of foods by nitrates, or nitrites used as a preservative in excess of 200 parts per million.
   2. Symptoms: Cyanosis, shock, lowered blood pressure, methemoglobinemia (hemoglobin in blood combines with nitrites instead of oxygen producing internal asphyxiation.)
   3. Onset of symptoms: 15 to 30 minutes.

H. Pesticides
   1. Occurence: Foods accidentally contaminated with pesticides.

VII. Dangerous Animals
   A. Shellfish
      1. Occurrence: Shellfish grown in polluted waters, if eaten raw, can cause typhoid fever, cholera, and infectious hepatitis.

15

DISEASE PREVENTION IN RESTAURANTS

WHAT ARE THE MOST FAVORABLE CONDITIONS FOR THE GROWTH OF DISEASE GERMS?

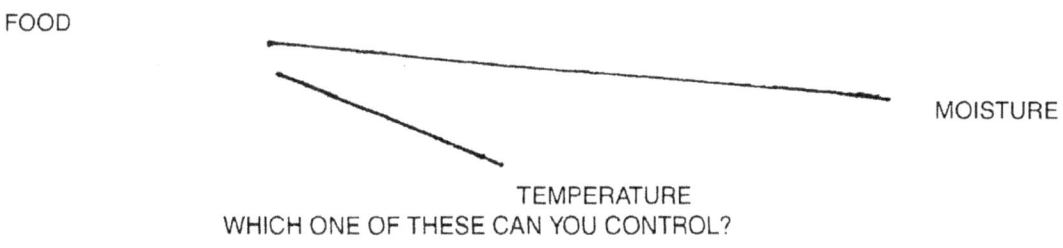

FOOD

MOISTURE

TEMPERATURE
WHICH ONE OF THESE CAN YOU CONTROL?

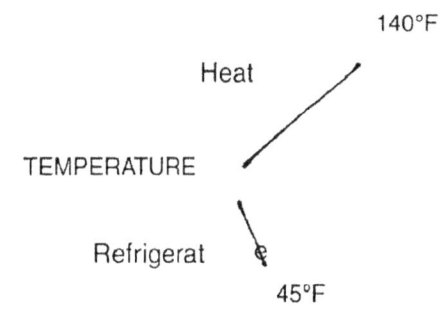

140°F
Heat
TEMPERATURE
Refrigerat
45°F

YOU CAN SPREAD DISEASE BY:

Carelessness
    Not washing hands before touching food, dishes, or utensils. Leaving food unprotected from dust, sneezes, rodents and insects. Using dirty equipment.
    Leaving food stand at room temperature.

Working when sick or with open sores
    Through food you infect.
    By direct contact with customers and fellow workers.
    By contaminating dishes and utensils.

YOU CAN GET DISEASE BY:
    Infection from a sick customer or fellow worker.
    Careless handling of soiled dishes.
    Eating infected food.
    Infection from rats, mice and insects.

FOOD PROTECTION

To Prevent Bacterial Food Poisoning and Infection
    Keep harmful bacteria out if possible.
    Keep them from growing if they do get in.
    How? By watching time and temperature, as well as cleanliness.

TIME
    Don't let food ready to serve stand longer than one hour at room temperature.

TEMPERATURE

Keep cold foods refrigerated at 45° F or lower until they are served.

Keep hot foods hot, above 140° F, until they are served.
WATCH THESE FOODS ESPECIALLY-BACTERIA LOVE THEM!
Cream filled or custard filled pastries, cakes and puddings.
Any dish made with cream sauce.
Meats, poultry and fish.
Dressing for poultry or meat.
Sandwiches, sandwich filling.

To Prevent Chemical Food Poisoning
Be sure all poisons are clearly labeled.
Never store poisons in food preparation areas.
Don't use insect sprays over or near food.
Don't keep any acid food or drink in a galvanized container.

SAFE STORAGE METHODS
Clean storage rooms, used for no other purpose.
All food stored at least six inches above floor.
Clean, neat refrigerator.
Food refrigerated in shallow containers, always covered.
Refrigerator shelves free of shelf-coverings.

SEVEN EASY RULES FOR SAFE FOOD
1. KEEP COLD FOODS COLD-HOT FOODS HOT. Don't let foods stand at room temperature.
2. KEEP HANDS CLEAN and touch food with hands as little as possible.
3. Don't let anyone with a skin infection or a cold handle food.
4. Keep kitchen, dining rooms and storage rooms free from rats, mice and insects.
5. Protect food from sneezes, customer handling, and dust.
6. Be sure poisons are well labeled and kept away from food preparation areas.
7. Wash dishes, glasses, silver and utensils by methods recommended by your health department.

FOOD SERVICE GLOSSARY

TABLE OF CONTENTS

	Page
Absorption Capability ... Antioxidant	1
Antipasti or Antipasto ... Bavarian	2
Beat ... Brown	3
Brunswick Stew ... Chili con Carne	4
Chill ... Croutons	5
Crullers ... Disinfectant	6
Disposables ... Éclair	7
Edible ... Fold	8
Fold In ... Fricassee	9
Fritters ... Goulash	10
Gourmet ... Horseshoes	11
Host ... Kebab	12
Knead ... Marinade	13
Marinate ... Mulligatawny	14
Myocide ... Pare	15
Parkerhouse Rolls ... Potable	16
Potentially Hazardous pH ... Reconstitute	17
Rehydrate ... Saponify	18
Saturation ... Skim	19
Slack Dough ... Steep	20
Sterilize ... Tartar	21
Tarts ... Truss	22
Vacuum Drying ... Zwieback	23

FOOD SERVICE GLOSSARY

A

ABSORPTION CAPABILITY
The property of flour to absorb and hold liquid.

ACIDITY
Sourness or tartness in a food product; in yeast doughs, a condition indicating excess fermentation; a factor in generating carbon dioxide for cake leavening.

AERATION
See LEAVENING.

AEROBIC BACTERIA
Those that require the presence of free oxygen as found in the air for growth.

A LA CARTE
On the menu alone, not in combination with a total meal.

A LA KING
A dish served with a cream sauce, usually containing green peppers and pimentos, and sometimes mushrooms and onions.

A LA MODE
In a fashion or the style of; for example, desserts served with ice cream or pot roast of beef cooked with vegetables.

ALBUMEN
Egg white.

AMBROSIA
A favorite southern dessert made of oranges, bananas, pineapple, and shredded coconut.

AMEBA
A simple animal-like organism that grows in water.

ANAEROBIC BACTERIA
Those that grow in oxygen-free atmosphere, deriving oxygen from solid or liquid materials and producing toxic substances.

ANTIBIOTICS
Substances produced by microorganisms and capable of inhibiting or killing other microorganisms.

ANTIOXIDANT
A chemical solution in which fruits and vegetables are dipped to prevent darkening.

ANTIPASTI or ANTIPASTO
An appetizer, or a spicy first course, consisting of relishes, cold sliced meats rolled with or without stuffings, fish, or other hors d'oeuvres eaten with a fork.

ANTISEPTIC
An agent that may or may not kill microorganisms, but does inhibit their growth. Peroxide is an example.

APPETIZER
A small portion of food or drink before or as the first course of a meal. These include a wide assortment of items ranging from cocktails, canapes, and hors d'oeuvres to plain fruit juices. The function of an appetizer is to pep up the appetite.

AU GRATIN
A thin surface crust formed by either bread or cheese, or both. Sometimes used with a cream sauce.

AU JUS
With natural juice. Roast rib au jus, for example, is beef served with unthickened gravy.

B

BACILLI
Cylindrical or rod-shaped bacteria responsible for such diseases as botulism, typhoid fever, and tuberculosis.

BACTERIA
Microscopic, one-cell microbes found in soil, water, and most material throughout nature. Some are responsible for disease and food spoilage, others are useful in industrial fermentation.

BACTERICIDE
Any substance that kills bacteria and related forms of life.

BAKE
To cook by dry heat in an oven. When applied to meats, it is called roasting.

BARBECUE
To roast or broil in a highly seasoned sauce.

BASTE
To moisten foods while cooking, especially while roasting meat. Melted fat, meat drippings, stock, water, or water and fat may be used.

BATTER
A homogeneous mixture of ingredients with liquid to make a mass that is of a soft plastic character.

BAVARIAN
A style of cooking that originated in the Bavarian section of Germany.

BEAT
To make a mixture smooth or to introduce air by using a lifting motion with spoon or whip.

BENCH TOLERANCE
The property of dough to ferment at a rate slow enough to prevent overfermentation while dough is being made up into units on the bench.

BLANCH
To rinse with boiling water, drain, and rinse in cold water. Used for rice, macaroni, and other pastas to prevent sticking. For potatoes, to cook in hot, deep fat for a short time until clear but not brown.

BLAND
Mild flavored, not stimulating to the taste.

BLEACHED FLOUR
Flour that has been treated by a chemical to remove its natural color and make it white.

BLEEDING
Dough that has been cut and left unsealed at the cut, thus permitting the escape of leavening gas. This term also applies to icing that bleeds.

BLEND
To mix thoroughly two or more ingredients.

BOIL
To cook in a liquid that bubbles actively during the time of cooking. The boiling temperature of water at sea level is 212° F.

BOTULISM
Acute food poisoning caused by botulin (toxin) in food.

BOUILLON
A clear soup made from beef or chicken stock or soup and gravy base.

BRAISE
To brown meat or vegetables in a small amount of fat, then to cook slowly, covered, at simmering temperature in a small amount of liquid. The liquid may be juices rendered from meat, or added water, milk, or meat stock.

BREAD
To coat with crumbs of bread or other food; or to dredge in seasoned flour, dip in a mixture of milk and slightly beaten eggs, and then dredge again in crumbs.

BROIL
To cook under or over direct heat.

BROWN
To cook, usually at medium or high heat, until the item of food darkens.

BRUNSWICK STEW
A main dish composed of a combination of poultry, meats, and vegetables.

BUTTERFLY
A method of cutting double chops (usually pork) from boneless loin strips. One side of each double chop is hinged together with a thin layer of meat.

BUTTERHORNS
Basic sweet dough cut and shaped like horns.

C

CACCIATORE
Chicken cooked "hunter" style. Browned chicken is braised in a sauce made with tomatoes, other vegetables, stock, and herbs.

CANAPE
Any of many varieties of appetizers, usually spread on bread, toast, or crackers and eaten with the fingers.

CANDY
To cook in sugar or syrup.

CARAMELIZED SUGAR
Dry sugar heated with constant stirring until melted and dark in color, used for flavoring and coloring.

CARBOHYDRATES
Sugars and starches derived chiefly from fruits and vegetable sources and containing set amounts of carbon, hydrogen, and oxygen.

CARBON DIOXIDE
A colorless, tasteless edible gas obtained during fermentation or from a combination of soda and acid.

CARRIERS
Persons who harbor and disseminate germs without having symptoms of a disease. The individual has either had the disease at one time and temporarily continues to excrete the organism, or has never manifested symptoms because of good resistance to the disease.

CHIFFONADE DRESSING
A salad dressing containing chopped hard-cooked eggs and beets.

CHIFFON CAKE
A sponge cake containing liquid shortening.

CHILI
A special pepper or its fruits. Dried, ground chili peppers are used in chili powder.

CHILI CON CARNE
Ground beef and beans seasoned with chili powder.

CHILL
 To place in a refrigerator or cool place until cold.

CHOP
 To cut into pieces with a knife or chopper.

CHOP SUEY
 A thick Chinese stew of thin slices of pork and various vegetables, such as bean sprouts, celery, and onions.

CLEAR FLOUR
 Lower grade and higher ash content flour remaining after the patent flour has been separated. (Used in rye bread.)

COAGULATE
 To thicken or form into a consistent mass.

COAT
 To cover the entire surface of food with a selected mixture.

CONDIMENTS
 Seasonings that in themselves furnish little nourishment, but which improve the flavor of food.

CONGEALING POINT
 Temperature or time at which a liquid changes to a firm or plastic condition.

COOKING LOSSES
 Loss of weight, liquid, or nutrients, and possibly a lowered palatability of a cooked food.

COOL
 To let stand, usually at room temperature, until no longer warm to touch.

CREAM
 To mix until smooth, sugar, shortening, and other ingredients; to incorporate air so that resultant mixture increases appreciably in volume and is thoroughly blended.

CREAM PUFFS
 Baked puffs of cream-puff dough, which are hollow; usually filled with cream pudding, whipped topping, or ice cream.

CREOLE
 A cooked sauce for poultry or shrimp. Usually served with rice.

CRISP
 To make somewhat firm and brittle.

CROUTONS
 Bread cut into small cubes and either fried or browned in the oven, according to the intended use. Used as a garnish, croutons are fried; as soup accompaniments, baked.

CRULLERS
Long, twisted doughnuts.

CRUMB
The soft part of bread or cake; a fragment of bread (see also BREAD).

CRUST
Hardened exterior of bread; pastry portion of pie.

CRUSTING
Formation of dry crust on the surface of doughs.

CUBE
To cut into approximately 1/4 to 1/2 inch squares.

CURDLE
To change into curd; to coagulate or thicken.

CURING
A form of processing meat, which improves its flavor and texture.

CURRY
A powder made from many spice ingredients and used as a seasoning for Indian and Oriental-type dishes, such as shrimp and chicken curry.

CUSTOM FOODS (RATION-DENSE)
Various types of labor- and space-saving foods, including canned, concentrated, dehydrated, frozen, and prefabricated items.

CUT IN (as for shortening)
To combine firm shortening and flour with pastry blender or knife.

D

DANISH PASTRY
A flaky yeast dough having butter or shortening rolled into it.

DASH
A scant 1/8 teaspoon.

DEVILED
A highly seasoned, chopped, ground, or whole mixture served hot or cold.

DICE
To cut into 1/4 inch or smaller cubes.

DISINFECTANT
A chemical agent that destroys bacteria and other harmful organisms.

DISPOSABLES
Disposable articles used for food preparation, eating, or drinking utensils, constructed wholly or in part from paper or synthetic materials and intended for one single service.

DISSOLVE
To mix a solid, dry substance with a liquid until the solid is in solution.

DIVIDER
A machine used to cut dough into a desired size or weight.

DOCKING
Punching a number of vertical impressions in a dough with a smooth round stick about the size of a pencil. Docking makes doughs expand uniformly without bursting during baking.

DOT
To place small pieces (usually butter) on the surface of food.

DOUGH
The thickened, uncooked mass of combined ingredients for bread, rolls, cookies, and pies, but usually applicable to bread.

DOUGH CONDITIONER
A chemical product added to flour to alter its properties to hold gas.

DOUGH TEMPERATURES
Temperature of dough at different stages of processing.

DRAIN
To remove liquid.

DREDGE
To sprinkle or coat with flour, sugar, or cornmeal.

DRIPPINGS
Fat and juice dripped from roasted meat.

DRY YEAST
A dehydrated form of yeast.

DU JOUR
Today's or of the day; for example, Specialite du jour — food specialty of the day.

DUSTING
Distributing a film of flour or starch on pans or work surfaces.

E

ECLAIR
A long, thin pastry made from cream puff batter, usually filled with cream pudding, whipped topping, or ice cream. The baked, filled shell is dusted with confectioner's sugar or covered with a thin layer of chocolate.

EDIBLE
Fit to eat, wholesome.

EMULSIFICATION
The process of blending together fat and water solutions of ingredients to produce a stable mixture that will not separate while standing.

ENCHILADAS
A dish consisting of tortillas, a sauce, a filling (cheese, meat, or beans) and garnished with a topping such as cheese, then rolled, stacked, or folded and baked.

ENRICHED BREAD
Bread made from enriched flour and containing federally prescribed amounts of thiamin, riboflavin, iron, and niacin.

ENTREE
An intermediary course of a meal, which in the United States is usually the "main" dish.

ENZYME
A substance, produced by living organisms, that has the power to bring about changes in organic materials.

EXTRACT
Essence of fruits or spices used for flavoring.

F

FAT ABSORPTION
Fat that is absorbed in food products as they are fried in deep fat.

FERMENTATION
The chemical changes of an organic compound caused by action of living organisms (yeast or bacteria), usually producing a leavening gas.

FILET
The English term is "fillet," designating a French method of dressing fish, poultry, or meat to exclude bones and include whole muscle strips.

FLIPPER
A can of food that bulges at one end, indicating food spoilage. If pressed, the bulge may "flip" to the opposite end. Can and contents should be discarded.

FOAM
Mass of beaten egg and sugar, as in sponge cake before the flour is added.

FOLD
To lap yeast dough over onto itself. With cake batter, to lift and lap the batter onto itself to lightly incorporate ingredients.

FOLD IN
To combine ingredients gently with an up-and-over motion by lifting one up through the other.

FOOD-CONTACT SURFACES
Those parts and areas of equipment and utensils with which food normally comes in contact. Also those surfaces with which food may come in contact and drain back into surfaces normally in contact with food.

FOOD INFECTION
A food-borne illness from ingesting foods carrying bacteria that later multiply within the body and produce disease.

FOOD INTOXICATION
Another term used synonymously with food poisoning, or the ingestion of a food containing a poisonous substance.

FOOD POISONING
A food-borne illness contracted through ingesting food that contains some poisonous substance.

FOOD VALUE
The quantity of a nutrient contained in a food substance.

FOO YOUNG
A popular dish made with scrambled eggs or omelets with cut Chinese vegetables, onions, and meat. Usually, the dish is served with a sauce.

FORMULA
A recipe giving ingredients, amounts to be used, and the method of preparing the finished product.

FRANCONIA POTATOES
Potatoes are parboiled, then oven-browned in butter.

FREEZE DRYING
Drying method where the product is first frozen and then placed within a vacuum chamber (freeze dehydration). Aided by small controlled inputs of thermal or microwave energy, the moisture in the product passes directly from the ice-crystalline state to moisture vapor that is evacuated.

FRENCH BREAD
A crusty bread, baked in a narrow strip and containing little or no shortening.

FRENCH FRY
To cook in deep fat.

FRICASSEE
To cook by braising; usually applied to fowl or veal cut into pieces.

FRITTERS
Fruit, meat, poultry, or vegetables that are dipped in batter and fried.

FRIZZLE
To cook in a small amount of fat until food is crisp and curled at the edges.

FRY
To cook in hot fat. When a small amount of fat is used, the process is known as pan-frying or sauteing; when food is partially covered, shallow frying; and when food is completely covered, deep-fat frying.

FUMIGANT
A gaseous or colloidal substance used to destroy insects or pests.

FUNGICIDE
An agent that destroys fungi.

G

GARNISH
To ornament or decorate food before serving.

GELATINIZE
To convert into a gelatinous or jelly-like form.

GERM
A pathogenic, or disease-producing bacteria. A small mass of living substance capable of developing into an organism or one of its parts.

GERMICIDE
A germ-destroying agent.

GIBLETS
The heart, gizzard, and liver of poultry cooked with water for use in preparing chicken or turkey stock or gravy.

GLAZE
A thick or thin sugar syrup or sugar mixture used to coat certain types of pastry and cakes.

GLUTEN
The elastic protein mass formed when the protein material of the wheat flour is mixed with water.

GOULASH
A Hungarian stew variously made in the United States of beef, veal, or frankfurters with onions and potatoes. The sauce has tomato paste and paprika as ingredients, served with sour cream if desired.

GOURMET
A connoisseur, or a critical judge, of good food and drink.

GRATE
To separate food into small pieces by rubbing it on a grater.

GREASE
To rub lightly with butter, shortening, or oil.

GRIDDLE
A flat surface or pan on which food is cooked by dry heat. Grease is removed as it accumulates. No liquid is added.

GRILL
See BROIL.

GRIND
To force food materials through a food chopper.

GUMBO
A Creole dish resembling soup, thickened somewhat with okra, its characteristic ingredient.

H

HARD SAUCE
A dessert sauce made of butter and confectioner's sugar, thoroughly creamed. The mixture is thinned or tempered with boiling water.

HASH
A baked dish made of chopped or minced meat and/or vegetables mixture in brown stock.

HEARTH
The heated baking surface of the floor of an oven.

HERMITS
A rich short-flake cookie.

HOLLANDAISE
A sauce made with egg yolks and butter and usually served over vegetables.

HONEY
A sweet syrupy substance produced by bees from flower nectar.

HORS D'OEUVRES
Light, snack-type foods eaten hot or cold at the beginning of a meal.

HORSESHOES
Danish pastry, shaped like horseshoes.

HOST
Any living animal or plant affording food for growth to a parasite.

HOT CROSS BUNS
Sweet, spicy, fruity buns with cross-cut on top, which usually is covered with a plain frosting.

HOT AIR DRYING
Products are cut in small pieces and spread on slat or wire bottom trays. Hot air is passed over and under trays to dry products.

HUMIDITY
The percent of moisture in air related to the total moisture capacity of that air at a particular temperature. Usually expressed as relative humidity.

HUNTER STYLE
Browned meat, usually chicken, braised in various combinations of tomatoes and other vegetables, stock, oil, garlic, and herbs.

HUSH PUPPIES
Deep-fried cornbread batter seasoned with onions. Used mostly in the South, usually with fish.

I

INCUBATION PERIOD
That time between entrance of disease-producing bacteria in a person and the first appearance of symptoms.

INSECTICIDE
Any chemical substance used for the destruction of insects.

ITALIENNE
Italian style of cooking.

J

JARDINIERE
A meat dish or garnish, "garden" style, made of several kinds of vegetables.

JULIENNE
A method of cutting meat, poultry, vegetables (especially potatoes), and fruits in long, thin strips.

K

KEBAB
Various Turkish-style dishes whose principal feature is skewered meat, usually lamb.

KNEAD
To work and press dough with the palms of the hands, turning and folding the dough at rapid intervals.

KOLACHES
A bread bun made from a soft dough and topped with fruit.

L

LACTIC ACID
An organic acid sometimes known as the acid of milk because it is produced when milk sours. Bacteria cause the souring.

LARDING
To cover uncooked lean meat or fish with strips of fat, or to insert strips of fat with a skewer.

LASAGNA
An Italian baked dish with broad noodles, or lasagna noodles, which has been cooked, drained, and combined in alternate layers with Italian meat sauce and cheese of two or three types (cottage, parmesan, and mozzarella).

LEAVENING
The aeration of a product (raising or lightening by air, steam, or gas (carbon dioxide)) that occurs during mixing and baking. The agent for generating gas in a dough or batter is usually yeast or baking powder.

LUKEWARM
Moderately warm or tepid.

LYONNAISE
A seasoning with onions originating in Lyons, France. Sauteed potatoes, green beans, and other vegetables are seasoned this way.

M

MAKEUP
Manual or mechanical manipulation of dough to provide a desired size and shape.

MARBLE CAKE
A cake of two or three colored batters partially mixed.

MARBLING
The intermingling of fat with lean in meat. Meat cut across the grain will show the presence or absence of marbling and may indicate its quality and palatability.

MARINADE
A preparation containing spices, herbs, condiments, vegetables, and a liquid (usually acid) in which a food is placed for a period of time to enhance its flavor, or to increase its tenderness.

MARINATE
To cover with dressing and allow to stand for a short length of time.

MARMALADE
A type of jam or preserve made with sliced fruits. Crushed fruits or whole fruits are used more commonly in jam.

MEAT SUBSTITUTE
Any food used as an entree that does not contain beef, veal, pork, or lamb. Some substitutes are protein-rich dishes such as eggs, fish, dried beans, and cheese.

MEDIA
The plural of medium.

MEDIUM
A material or combination of materials used for cultivation of microorganisms.

MELTING POINT
The temperature at which a solid becomes a liquid.

MERINGUE
A white frothy mass of beaten egg whites and sugar.

MILK FAT
The fat in milk and milk products.

MILK LIQUID
Fresh fluid milk or evaporated or powdered milk reconstituted to the equivalent of fresh fluid milk.

MINCE
To cut or chop into very small pieces, using knife or chopper.

MINESTRONE
Thickened vegetable soup containing lentils or beans.

MIXING
To unite two or more ingredients.

MOCHA
A flavor combination of coffee and chocolate, but predominately that of coffee.

MOLD
Microscopic, multicellular, thread-like fungi growing on moist surfaces of organic material.

MOLDER
Machine that shapes dough pieces for various shapes.

MULLIGATAWNY
A soup with a chicken-stock base highly seasoned, chiefly by curry powder.

MYOCIDE
An agent that destroys molds.

N

NUTRIENT
A food substance that humans require to support life and health.

O

O'BRIEN
A style of preparing sauteed vegetables with diced green peppers and pimientos.

OLD DOUGHS
Overfermented yeast dough that produces a finished baked loaf, dark in crumb color, sour in flavor, low in volume, coarse in grain, and tough in texture.

OMELET
Eggs beaten to a froth, cooked with stirring until set, and served in a half-round form by folding one half over the other.

OVEN
A chamber used for baking, heating, or drying.

OYSTER MUSCLE
Tender, oval piece of dark poultry meat found in the recess on either side of the back.

P

PALATABLE
Agreeable to the palate or taste.

PAN BROIL
See BROIL.

PAN FRY
See FRY.

PARASITES
Organisms that live in or on a living host.

PARBOIL
To boil in water until partially cooked.

PARE
To trim and remove all superfluous matter from any article.

PARKERHOUSE ROLLS
Folded buns of fairly rich dough.

PARMESAN
A very hard, dry cheese with a sharp flavor.

PASTA (or PASTE)
Any macaroni product, including spaghetti, noodles, and the other pastas.

PATHOGENS
Disease-producing microorganisms.

PEEL
To remove skin, using a knife or peeling machine.

PEPPER POT
Any of a wide variety of styles of highly seasoned soup or stew.

PICKLE
A method of preserving food by a salt and water (or vinegar) solution.

PILAF
An oriental or Turkish dish made of rice cooked in beef or chicken stock and mildly flavored with onions.

PIQUANT
A tart, pleasantly sharp flavor. A piquant sauce or dressing contains lemon juice or vinegar.

PIT
To remove pits or seeds (as from dates or avocados).

PLASTICITY
The consistency or feel of shortening.

POACH
Method of cooking food in a hot liquid that is kept just below the boiling point.

POLONAISE
A garnish consisting of chopped egg and parsley served on cauliflower, asparagus, or other dishes. Bread crumbs are sometimes added.

PPM
Parts per million.

PORCUPINE
A preparation of ground beef and rice shaped into balls and cooked in tomato sauce.

POTABLE
Suitable for drinking.

POTENTIALLY HAZARDOUS pH
Any perishable food which consists in whole or in part of milk or milk products, eggs, meat, poultry, fish, shellfish, synthetic food, or other ingredient capable of supporting rapid and progressive growth of pathogens.

PREHEAT
To heat to the desired baking temperature before placing food in the oven.

PROOF BOX
A tightly closed box or cabinet equipped with shelves to permit the introduction of heat and steam; used for fermenting dough.

PROOFING PERIOD
The time between molding and baking during which dough rises.

PROTOZOA
Minute, one-celled animals.

PROVOLONE
A cured, hard cheese that has a smoky flavor.

PSYCHROPHILIC BACTERIA
Microorganisms that grow at temperatures near freezing.

PUREE
The pulp of a boiled food that has been rubbed through a sieve. Soup is called puree when it has been thickened with its sieved, pulpy ingredients.

Q

QUICK BREADS
Bread products baked from a lean, chemically leavened batter.

R

RABBIT OR RAREBIT
A melted-cheese dish.

RAGOUT
The French word for "stew."

RANCID
A disagreeable odor or flavor. Usually used to describe foods with high fat content, when oxidation occurs.

READY-TO-COOK POULTRY
Drawn or eviscerated poultry.

RECONSTITUTE
To restore the water taken from a food when it was dehydrated.

REHYDRATE
Combining a food with the same quantity of water that has been removed from it (see also RECONSTITUTE).

RELISH
A side dish, usually contrasting in color, shape, and texture to the meal. Usually designed to add flavor, zest, and interest to a meal.

RISSOLE
A French term meaning to obtain a crackling food by means of heat. Rissole potatoes are cooked to a golden brown crispness in fat.

ROAST
See BAKE.

ROPE
A spoiling bacterial growth in bread experienced when the dough becomes infected with bacterial spores. Poor sanitation can result in rope.

ROUNDING OR ROUNDING UP
Shaping of dough pieces into a ball to seal end and prevent bleeding and escape of gas.

ROUX
Preparation of flour and melted butter (or fat) used to thicken sauces, gravies, and soups.

ROYAL FROSTING
Decorative frosting of cooked sugar and egg whites.

S

SAFE HOLDING TEMPERATURE
A range of cold and hot temperatures considered safe for holding potentially hazardous foods, including those refrigeration temperatures 40° F, or below, or heating temperatures 140° F, or above.

SALISBURY STEAK
A ground meat dish cooked with onions and made to resemble steak in shape. Sometimes referred to as hamburg steak.

SALMONELLA INFECTION
A type of food poisoning transmitted through foods such as poultry and poultry products containing salmonella bacteria.

SANITIZE
Effective bactericidal treatment of clean surfaces of equipment and utensils by an established process that is effective in destroying microorganisms.

SAPONIFY
To convert to soap.

SATURATION
Absorption to the limit of the capacity.

SAUERBRATEN
A beef pot roast cooked in a sour sauce variously prepared with spices and vinegar, and sometimes served with sour cream.

SAUTE
See FRY.

SCALD
To heat a liquid over hot water or direct heat to a temperature just below the boiling point.

SCALE
An instrument for weighing.

SCALING
Apportioning batter or dough according to unit of weight.

SCALLOP
To bake food, usually cut in pieces, with a sauce or other liquid.

SCORE
To cut shallow slits or gashes in the surface of food with a knife.

SCORING
Judging finished goods according to points of perfection; or to cut or slash the top surface of dough pieces.

SEASON
To add, or sprinkle, with seasonings or condiments.

SHRED
To cut or tear into thin strips or pieces using a knife or a shredder attachment.

SIFTING
Passing through fine sieve for effective blending and to remove foreign or oversize particles.

SIMMER
To cook in liquid at a temperature just below the boiling point.

SKEWER
A sharp metal or wood pin used to hold parts of poultry meat or skin together while being roasted.

SKIM
To remove floating matter from the surface of a liquid with a spoon, ladle, or skimmer.

SLACK DOUGH
This is a dough that is soft and extensible but has lost its resiliency.

SLIVER
To cut or split into long, thin pieces.

SMOKING
A treatment used on most cured meat to add color and flavor.

SMORGASBORD
A Scandinavian-type luncheon or supper, served buffet style. Many different dishes are served, including hot and cold hors d'oeuvres, pickled vegetables, fish, assorted cheeses, jellied salads, cold and hot fish, and meats.

SMOTHER
To cook in a covered container, as smothered onions.

SNAPS
Small cookies that run flat during baking and become crisp on cooking.

SNICKERDOODLE
A coffeecake with a crumb topping.

SOLIDIFYING POINT
Temperature at which a fluid changes to a solid.

SPORE
Any one of various small or minute primitive reproductive bodies, capable of maintaining and reproducing itself. These are unicellular, produced by plants, molds, and bacteria.

SPRAY DRYING
Used for liquids and thick materials such as soup. Hot air coming into a drier contacts the small globules of the product and causes the water to be evaporated.

SPRINGER
A marked bulging of a food can at one or both ends. Improper exhausting of air from the can before sealing, or bacterial or chemical growth may cause swelling and spoilage.

SPRINKLE
To scatter in drops or small particles, such as chopped parsley, over a finished product.

STAPHYLOCOCCI
A family of bacteria formed in grapelike clusters, living as parasites on the outer skin and mucous membrane.

STEAM
To cook in steam with or without pressure.

STEEP
To let stand in hot liquid below boiling temperature to extract flavor, color, or other qualities from a specific food.

STERILIZE
To destroy microorganisms by chemical or mechanical means.

STEW
To simmer in liquid.

STIR
To blend or mix ingredients by using a spoon or other implement.

STREPTOCOCCI
Single-celled, globular-shaped bacteria.

STROGANOFF
Beef prepared with sour cream.

STRONG FLOUR
One that is suitable for the production of bread of good volume and quality.

SUCCOTASH
A combination of corn and lima beans.

SUGAR
To sprinkle or mix with sugar; refers to granulated unless otherwise specified in recipe.

SUKIYAKI
A popular Japanese dish consisting of thin slices of meat fried with onions and other vegetables, including bean sprouts, and soy sauce containing seasoning, herbs, and spices.

SWELLER
A can of food having both ends bulging as a result of spoilage. Swellers should be discarded, except molasses, in which this condition is normal in a warm climate.

T

TABLEWARE
A general term referring to multi use eating and drinking utensils, including knives, forks, spoons, and dishes.

TACO
An open-face sandwich, Mexican style, made of fried tortillas shaped like a shell and filled with a hot meat-vegetable mixture.

TAMALE
A highly seasoned steamed dish made of cornmeal with ground beef or chicken rolled in the center.

TARTAR
A rich sauce made with salad dressing, onions, parsley, and sometimes pickle relish, olives, and cucumbers, served with fish and shellfish.

TARTS
Small pastries with heavy fruit or cream filling.

TEMPERING
Adjusting temperature of ingredients to a certain degree.

TETRAZINNI
An Italian dish with chicken, green peppers, and onions mixed in spaghetti and served with shredded cheese.

TEXTURE
The quality of the interior structure of a baked product. Usually sensed by the touch of the cut surface as well as by sight and taste.

THERMOSTAT
A device for maintaining constant temperature.

THICKEN
To transform a thin liquid into a thick one either by the gelatinization of flour starches or the coagulation of egg protein.

TOAST
To brown the surface of a food by the application of direct heat.

TORTILLA
A Mexican bread made with white corn flour and water. Special techniques are used in handling the dough to roll it thin as a pie crust. It is baked on an ungreased griddle or in the oven.

TOSS
To lightly mix one or more ingredients. Usually refers to salad ingredients.

TOXIN
A waste product, given off by an organism causing contamination of food and subsequent illness in human beings. It is the toxin of a disease-producing germ that causes the poisoning.

TRICHINOSIS
A food-borne disease transmitted through pork containing a parasite, Trichinella spirallis, or its larvae, which infects animals.

TROUGHS
Large containers, usually on wheels, used for holding large masses of raising dough.

TRUSS
To bind or fasten together the wings and legs of poultry with the aid of string or metal skewers.

V

VACUUM DRYING
Vacuum is applied to liquids and fills the liquid with bubbles, creating a puffing effect. The puffed product is then dried, leaving a solid fragile mass. This is then crushed to reduce bulk.

VERMICELLI
A pasta, slightly yellow in color, shaped like spaghetti and very thin.

VINAIGRETTE
A mixture of oil and vinegar seasoned with salt, pepper, and herbs, used in sauces and dressings.

VIRUS
A group of organisms of ultramicroscopic size that grow in living tissue and may produce disease in animals and plants. Viruses are smaller than bacteria and, hence, pass through membranes or filters.

W

WASH
A liquid brushed on the surface of an unbaked or baked product (may be water, milk, starch solution, thin syrup, or egg).

WATER ABSORPTION
Water required to produce a bread dough of desired consistency. Flours vary in ability to absorb water, depending on the age of the flour, moisture content, wheat from which it is milled, storage conditions, and milling process.

WHEY
Liquid remaining after the removal of fat, casein, and other substances from milk.

WHIP
To beat rapidly to increase volume by incorporating air.

Y

YEAST
A group of small, single-celled plants, oval in shape and several times larger than bacteria. Yeast helps to promote fermentation and is useful in producing bread, cheese, wine, and so on.

YOUNG DOUGHS
Underfermented yeast dough producing finished yeast goods that are light in color, tight in grain, and low in volume (heavy).

Z

ZWIEBACK
A toast made of bread or plain coffeecake dried in slow oven.

www.ingramcontent.com/pod-product-compliance
Lightning Source LLC
Chambersburg PA
CBHW081809300426
44116CB00014B/2292